# EASY EXPERIMENTS IN ELEMENTARY SCIENCE

# EASY EXPERIMENTS IN ELEMENTARY SCIENCE

by

*Herbert McKay*

YESTERDAY'S CLASSICS

ITHACA, NEW YORK

This edition, first published in 2021 by Yesterday's Classics, an imprint of Yesterday's Classics, LLC, is an unabridged republication of the text originally published by Oxford University Press in 1922. For the complete listing of the books that are published by Yesterday's Classics, please visit www.yesterdaysclassics.com. Yesterday's Classics is the publishing arm of Gateway to the Classics which presents the complete text of hundreds of classic books for children at www.gatewaytotheclassics.com.

ISBN: 978-1-63334-147-0

Yesterday's Classics, LLC
PO Box 339
Ithaca, NY 14851

# PREFACE

This book is a first book in science, intended for pupils of any age, but the younger the better.

Easy experiments without the use of formal apparatus can be repeated at home.

Any child of eight can do most of the experiments in this book. Some of them were devised by my own boy before he was eight. He derived more amusement from them than ordinary toys.

Pupils will be able to devise new easy experiments for themselves. They will begin to question nature. A more difficult series of experiments would not develop this attitude of mind. Such experiments have a tendency to keep science strictly to the science lesson.

Easy experiments help children to understand the science of everyday life. The direction of smoke in the air, a cap blown off by the wind, sugar dissolving in hot tea, are examples of everyday phenomena which may be developed by easy reasoning into sound science training.

Easy experiments and easy reasoning based on them form an ideal educational subject for little children. So far from being abstruse, as it is often wrongly supposed to be, easy science is practical and straightforward. The results of experiments are obvious to the senses. The reasoning is no more than a little common sense.

A glance at the summaries will show that pupils who do the easy experiments are acquiring a considerable amount of scientific knowledge and training.

H. McKay

# CONTENTS

# CONTENTS

# HINTS ON
# HOME-MADE APPARATUS

i. Nearly all the apparatus used in the easy experiments in this book is either familiar household things or can be easily made.

ii. Experiments have been chosen which can be carried out either at school or at home.

iii. A simple and useful laboratory may be made at home with little or no expense. Tin cans and jam jars are very useful. A large basin can always be borrowed from the kitchen.

iv. Spring balances are a cheap form of weighing machine. It is well to have two—one weighing up to a pound, and the other to a stone or half a stone.

v. At home heating can be done over a small gas-ring. At school it is well to have a Bunsen burner.

vi. The following are useful: a six-inch square of fine wire gauze; pieces of looking-glass, especially oblong pieces; small sheets of coloured glass; triangular glass prisms (these are made for a sort of ornament. They serve a much higher purpose when used for experiments on light); a lamp chimney; a magnifying glass; some lengths of glass tubing.

vii. **A measuring jar**. Get a tall glass jar—a gas jar or a preserved fruit jar. Gum a strip of paper on the outside from top to bottom. (Figure 1.)

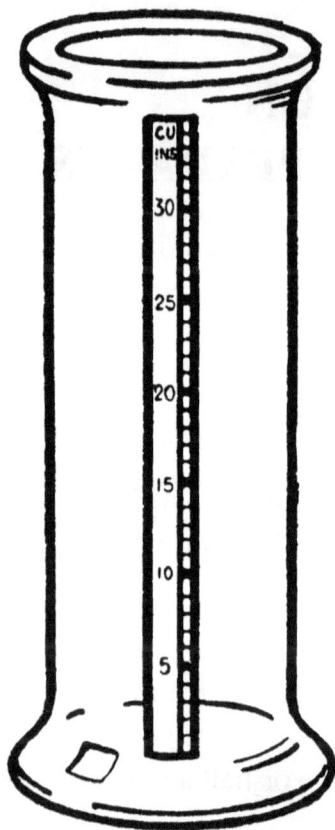

Cut a piece of wood as accurately as you can one inch square, and longer than the jar. Mark the wood accurately in inches, so that each part is a cubic inch.

Hold the wood upright in the jar touching the bottom, and pour in water till it reaches the highest inch mark that is inside the jar. Mark the level of the water on the strip of paper.

Withdraw, say, five cubic inches and mark the level again. Then withdraw five cubic inches again and mark the level.

**Fig 1**

Hold the wood again upright and touching the bottom. Fill the jar with water up to the lowest mark. Withdraw five cubic inches again. In this way carrying the markings as low as possible.

The marking may be completed by measurement. It is well never to use the lowest part of the jar.

viii. **A scale-pan**. Scale-pans are often needed.

Get a tin lid and make three nail-holes equally spaced round the brim. Tie pieces of thin string in these holes and knot them together above. (Figure 2.)

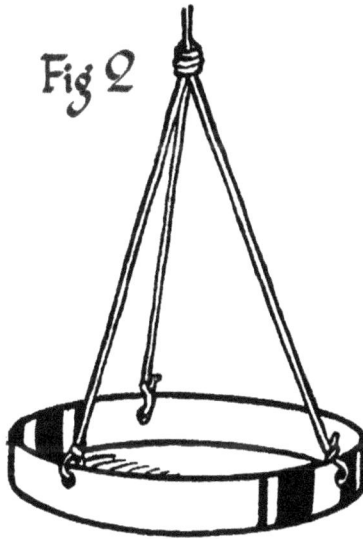

Fig 2

# CHAPTER I

# LESSONS ON THE AIR

### 1. *How we know there is air*

**Experiment 1.** Swing 'round your arm with the palm flat. The air can be felt. You feel it also when it blows against you, and when you run through it.

**Experiment 2.** Take a deep breath and blow some scraps of paper on the table. You can see the air moving the papers.

**Experiment 3.** If there is a small room with a door opening outward, close the windows and any other openings. Then open the door and try to close it quickly. The cushioning effect of the air can be felt.

Repeat this experiment with a window open. The cushioning effect is lost because air escapes through the window. This can be shown by holding smouldering brown paper near the open window while some one else shuts the door quickly.

**Experiment 4.** Drop a sheet of thin paper and notice that it seems to be supported.

**Experiment 5.** Hold an "empty" bottle mouth

downward in a basin of water. You will see that the water does not rush into the bottle. It is kept out by the air in the bottle.

Gradually tilt the bottle. Bubbles of air are seen escaping. As they escape water runs into the bottle.

**Experiment 6.** Hold a finger tightly over the end of a piece of glass tubing. Then hold the tubing upright in water. It will be seen that water does not enter the tube.

Take the finger from the end of the tube. Air can be felt escaping, and water rises in the tube.

**Experiment 7.** Fill a glass tumbler with water and upend it in a basin of water. In doing this keep the open end down and slowly raise the closed end. (Figure 3.)

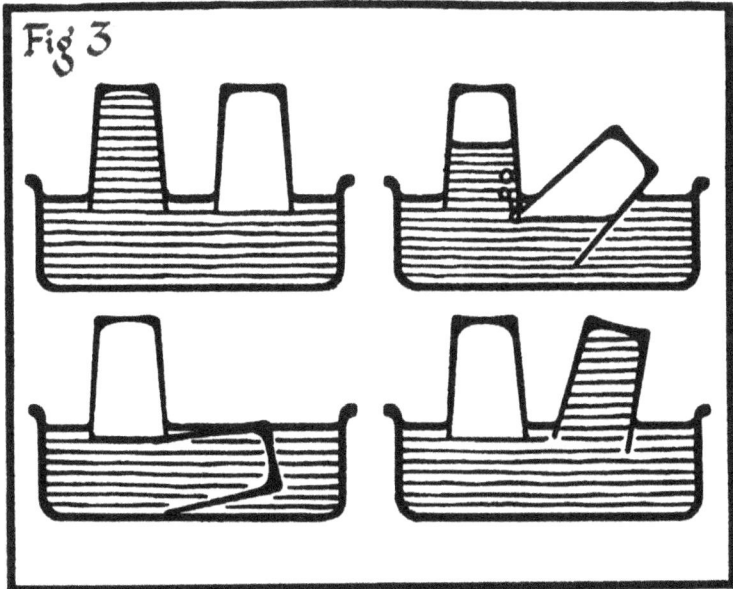

Fig 3

Hold a second tumbler beside the first, but without water in it.

Now tilt the second tumbler slightly with its rim under the rim of the first tumbler. Bubbles of air can be seen rising into the first tumbler.

With care the whole of the air can be poured into the first tumbler, and the second tumbler is then seen to be full of water.

**Experiment 8.** Hold a sheet of cardboard in the hand and swing it through the air edge on. You will find that the air offers very little resistance to the movement.

Now swing the cardboard round held upright. You will find that the resistance of the air is much greater.

**Experiment 9.** Repeat the last experiment, using sheets of cardboard of different sizes from six inches square up to two feet square (or the largest piece you can get).

You will find that the larger the sheet is, the greater is the resistance of the air.

**Experiment 10.** Hold a sheet of paper flat on the hand. Run along, gradually turning the hand over till the sheet of paper is being held up against the hand by the air pressing on it.

As soon as you stop, the paper drops.

**Experiment 11.** When you are flying a kite draw it rapidly against the air. You will see that the kite is pushed up by the air.

If there is no wind you will find that the kite begins to fall as soon as you stop pulling it against the air.

Try to fly a kite by pulling it in the same direction

as the wind. Then notice the difference when you pull against the wind so as to get the full pressure of the moving air.

## *2. Air presses on things*

It is rather difficult to detect the pressure of the air because usually air pressure in one direction is balanced by an equal air pressure in the opposite direction.

The pressure on one side of a door, for example, is usually balanced by the pressure on the other side. We do not notice the pressure at all.

But in coal mines, where air is driven down for ventilation, the air pressure is sometimes greater on one side of a door than on the other. It is then difficult to open the door against the pressure. Such doors usually have a hole in them with a slide over it. Before opening the door, the hole is opened. Air rushes through and equalizes the pressure on the two sides of the door. The door then opens easily.

In the following experiments it will be seen that air pressure on one side of a thing is reduced to show the effect of the air pressure on the other side.

**Experiment 1.** Fill a glass tumbler with water and upend it in a basin of water. Slip a piece of paper (a little larger than the mouth of the tumbler) over the tumbler. Hold it there on the flat hand. (Figure 4.)

Raise the tumbler out of the water. Take care that the paper is still flat over the mouth. Remove the hand

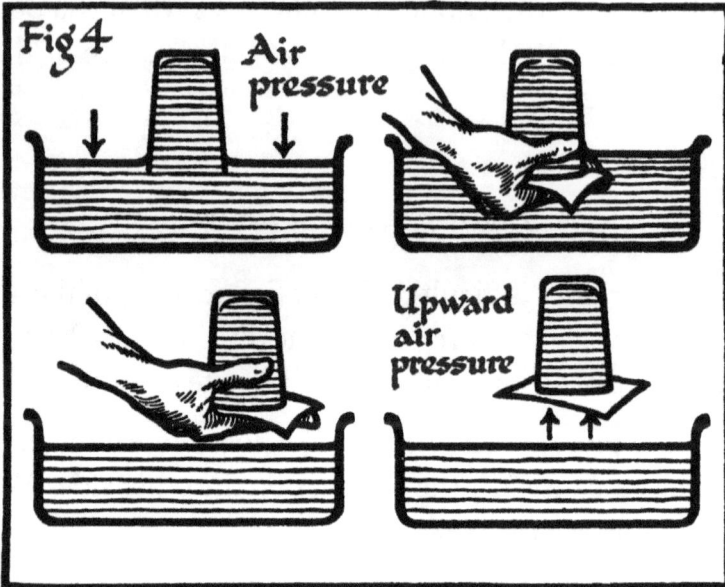

Fig 4. Air pressure / Upward air pressure

holding the paper up. It will be found that the paper and the water in the tumbler are held up by the air pressing up on the paper.

The upward pressure of the air is greater than the downward pressure of the water in the tumbler.

**Experiment 2.** Make a nail-hole in the bottom of a tin can, and another in the side.

Fill the tin with water and fit the lid on tightly. Hold the tin over a basin of water. Cover the hole in the side with a finger. You will find that the water does not run out. It is kept in by the air pressing up.

Open the hole in the side. The water begins to run out at once because the upward pressure of the air is balanced by the downward pressure of air which gets into the tin through the hole in the side.

Open and close the hole in the side several times, and note how the flow of water starts and stops.

**Experiment 3.** Cut out a round piece of leather. Make a nail-hole in the middle. Pass a piece of strong string through the hole and knot it below.

Leave the leather to soak in water for at least a day.

Put the sucker on a flat piece of stone or wood. Press it down tightly to squeeze out the air from underneath it. The stone or wood may then be raised by the string. The sucker is held down by the pressure of air above it which is not balanced by air pressure below it.

Slip a knife under the sucker. It comes away instantly because air gets in below it.

Press the sucker to a smooth wall and pull at the string to show the sideways pressure of air. The sucker may also be pressed to flat surfaces leaning in any direction.

**Experiment 4.** Place a plate or a flat piece of tin on the table. Cut a potato in two and press a cut surface of the potato tightly on the plate. When the air has been squeezed out from under the potato the plate may be raised by means of the potato.

**Experiment 5.** Place a thin strip of wood sticking half its length over the edge of the table. Spread a newspaper flat over the part of the wood on the table.

Press the end of the wood gently. The newspaper is raised.

Now give the end of the wood a sharp blow. If you

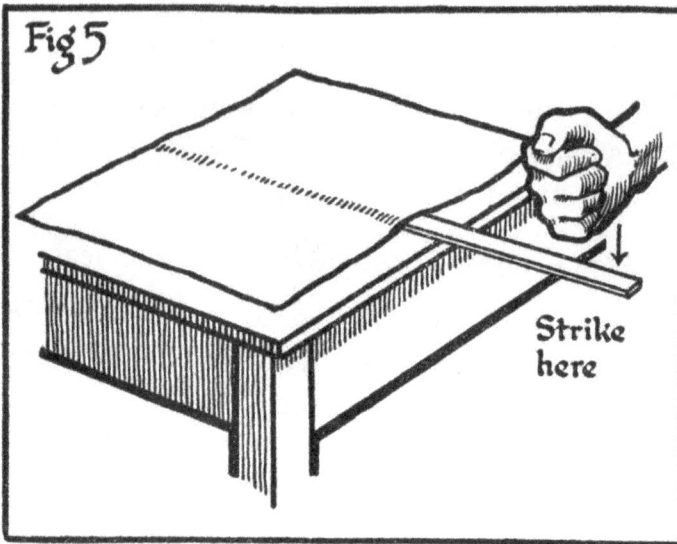

Fig 5

Strike here

strike sharply enough the strip of wood may break. (Figure 5.)

When you press gently, the air has time to get in under the paper to balance the air pressure above. When you strike sharply the pressure above is not balanced for a moment by air pressure below, and the wood is held down long enough for it to be broken.

**Experiment 6.** (*Note:* For this experiment use narrow tubing or wider tubing drawn out narrow at the end.) Hold a straight piece of glass tubing upright in water. Put a finger over the upper end and raise the tubing out of the water.

So long as the finger is kept in its place the water does not run out. It is kept in by the upward pressure of the air below. Remove the finger and the water runs out. The air pressure below is now balanced by the air pressure above.

A tube may be used in this way to carry small amounts of water from one jar to another.

## 3. *Air pressure*

**Experiment 1.** Fill a tumbler with water and upend it in a basin of water. Notice how the water is held up in the tumbler. The air pressing down on the flat surface of the water presses it up into the tumbler.

**Experiment 2.** Fill a tumbler with water and upend it in a basin of water. Pass a piece of tubing (rubber tubing or bent glass tubing) under the water and up to the top of the tumbler. (Figure 6.)

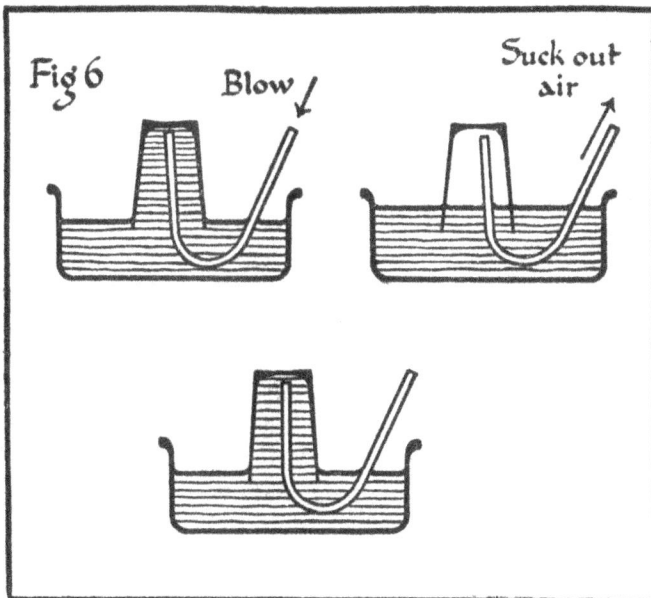

Blow down the tube. As soon as air reaches the top of the tumbler the water drops to the level of the water outside. The air pressure inside is now equal to that outside.

Increase the air pressure in the tumbler by blowing down the tube. The water begins to fall in the tumbler.

Reduce the air pressure in the tumbler by sucking air out of the tube. The water begins to rise in the tumbler. You may notice that if you leave the tube open before the water has risen to the end of it, the water at once sinks to the level of the water outside.

**Experiment 3.** Use a syringe to raise water out of a basin. Notice how the air pressure in the syringe is reduced by raising the plunger.

**Experiment 4.** Use a fountain-pen filler to raise ink. The air pressure is reduced by squeezing the rubber and then allowing it to expand.

**Experiment 5.** Get a cork that will fit a soda-water bottle. Make a hole in the cork and push a piece of glass tubing through it. (If you have no other way of making a hole in the cork, use a large nail.)

Nearly fill the bottle with water, push the cork in, and see that the end of the tube is about two inches above the cork. (Figure 7.)

Hold the bottle cork down over a basin of water and notice exactly what happens. A little water runs out. This reduces the pressure above and air rushes in from below. This increases the pressure above and more water runs out. The process goes on till the bottle is empty.

**Experiment 6.** Fill a narrow-necked bottle with

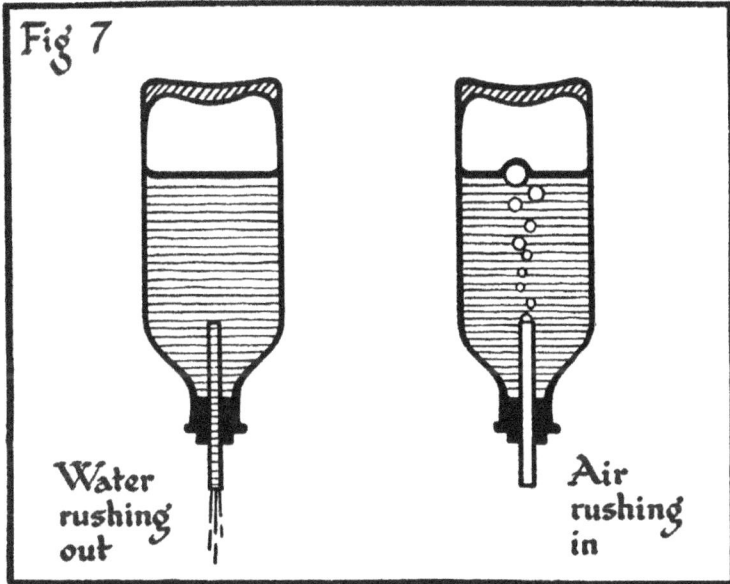

Fig 7

Water rushing out

Air rushing in

water, upend it over a basin, and watch how the water runs out. You should be able to see that the process is the same as when a narrow tube was used. It may, however, be a little more irregular.

**Experiment 7.** Rubber tubing or a piece of bent glass tubing may be used as a siphon.

Place a jar of water in a raised position (for example, on a wooden box placed on the table). Place another jar below to catch the water that comes over.

Fill the tube with water by placing it in a basin of water or by sucking water into it. Close each end of the tube with a finger. Put one end of the tube into the jar of water and lower the other end over the jar below.

Open the ends of the tube. Water will be seen to run out so long as the ends of the tube are below the level of the water surface.

Let the water go on running till it stops. Find out why it stops.

You might also try to raise water to a higher level by siphoning. You will soon find that you cannot.

If there were no air pressure the water in the bent tube would simply run out on either side. The air pressures at the ends of the tube balance, but in the longer limb there is a greater length of water pressing down, so the water runs down at that side.

**Experiment 8.** If you have a bottle of preserved fruit you will find that the lid is tightly fixed on. Make a small hole in the lid and it comes off at once.

The lid is placed in position when the top of the bottle is full of steam. When the bottle cools the lid is held down by the pressure of the air.

**Experiment 9.** Blow into a football bladder or a toy balloon. Notice that it fills out evenly, showing that the pressure of the air is the same in all directions.

The same even effect may be noted when air is pumped into a bicycle tyre.

### 4. Air is elastic

**Experiment 1.** Fill a narrow-necked bottle one-quarter full of water. Blow hard into the bottle and at once close it with your thumb. Tilt the bottle till the mouth is under water. Then open the mouth slightly. Water will be sent squirting out. After a little practice you will find that you can squirt it some distance. (Figure 8.)

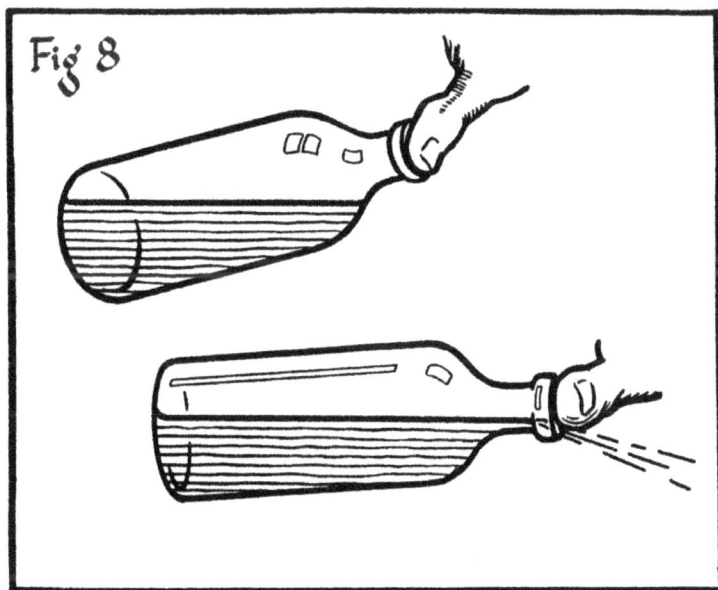

Fig 8

When you blow into the bottle the air in the bottle is compressed. As soon as you remove your thumb it springs back to its former size and so drives out the water.

The pressure of compressed air is used to drive machines, especially in coal-mines where steam or oil would be dangerous.

**Experiment 2.** Wet an india-rubber ball and throw it on the floor. You will find a round wet mark where it hits the floor. This shows that the ball was squeezed up or compressed when it hit the floor. To see the amount of squeezing, put the ball on the mark and press it down till it just fits on the mark.

The ball jumps back because the compressed air at once springs back to its former size. To show that this is so drop two balls together, one with a hole and the other without. If the hole is at all big the ball bounces very feebly.

**Experiment 3.** Close the end of a garden syringe. (This can be done with clay or plasticine.) Then ram the plunger down hard and let go.

You will feel the cushioning effect of the air. When you let go the plunger it will be driven back by the spring of the compressed air.

**Experiment 4.** Blow out a toy balloon and close the opening. Press the balloon gently with the fingers. It gives way but recovers its shape when the pressure is removed.

The same effect may be noted with an india-rubber ball.

**Experiment 5.** If any kind of pop-gun is available use it and find out how it works. You will find that air is compressed and then suddenly released. It quickly recovers its former size and drives before it the cork or whatever was put in its way.

**Experiment 6.** Get a bottle with a long straight neck and a cork to fit it.

Fill the bottle nearly full of water. Try to push in the cork. You will find that the air pushes it back.

**Experiment 7.** If there is a small room with a door opening outward close all the openings and repeat the experiment of trying to close the door quickly.

You will feel the cushioning effect of the air. This effect is used in air-cushions of various kinds. Pneumatic tyres are a kind of air-cushion. Watch a bicycle moving slowly. You will see that the tyres give slightly where they touch the ground and at once recover their shape.

**Experiment 8.** On a calm day close all the openings in a room except one window. Pin some thin strips of paper so that they hang across the opening.

Jerk the door open five or six inches. The shock is carried through the air and the streamers are pushed out almost instantly. Jerk the door back and the streamers are pushed in by the air outside.

Note that the pressure of the door on the air is carried to every part of the room. The effect is seen at the windows because the streamers show it there.

### 5. Things need air to burn

**Experiment 1.** Light a candle, place it on the table, and put a large glass jar over it. Notice that the candle soon goes out.

Repeat the experiment. Just as the candle is going out raise the jar to admit more air. The candle will burn up again.

**Experiment 2.** Try other methods of cutting off the supply of air.

Set fire to a piece of sulphur on a tin lid. Then cover the burning sulphur with sand.

Set fire to another piece of sulphur and cover it with a piece of wood or tin for a short time.

**Experiment 3.** Try to set fire to the pages of an old magazine. You will find it difficult because the pages are so close together that there is little air between them.

Now raise the pages one by one to admit air, and they burn readily. Or crumple the pages.

**Experiment 4.** Set fire to a sheet of paper. Try to put it out by waving it about. It burns better because it is continually being brought to fresh air.

Now lay a sheet of burning paper flat on the table or the floor. The paper burns badly or goes out because very little air can get to it.

**Experiment 5.** Make a small fire of crumpled paper on the ground. Cut off the supply of air by putting an old rug or mat over it.

This is the method to use if your clothes should catch fire. Do not feed the fire by rushing into fresh air, but smother it by cutting off the supply of air.

**Experiment 6.** Fix two candles upright on the bottom of a basin of water. (One candle should be longer than the other.) (Figure 9.)

Light the candles and place a jar over them. The candles soon go out. Leave the jar to cool. When the jar is cold you will see that water has risen into it showing that some of the air has been used up.

Slip a piece of cardboard over the mouth of the jar, raise it out of the water, and turn it mouth up and

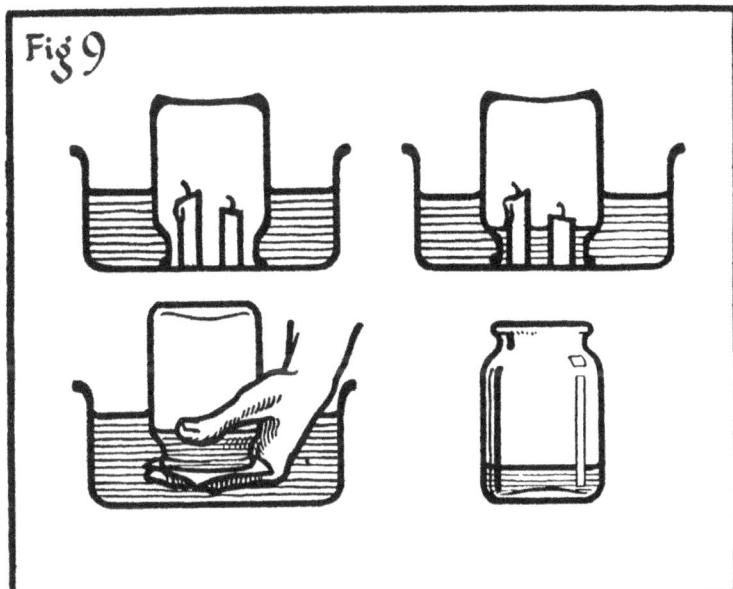

Fig 9

still covered. Light a taper or a paper spill, remove the cardboard cover, and put the taper into the jar. The taper goes out at once. It will not burn in the gas left.

The part of the air which makes things burn is called oxygen. The remainder (in which a taper does not burn) is chiefly nitrogen.

**Experiment 7.** Rinse a glass jar (a jam jar) with water. Sprinkle the inside with iron filings. Upend the jar in a basin of water and place a weight on it to keep it steady. Treat other jars in the same way.

Watch the jars day by day. You will see that water gradually rises in them and then ceases to rise.

Take one jar out of the water and plunge a lighted taper or spill into it. The taper goes out at once.

Measure the amount of water that has risen into

one of the jars. (Either use a measuring jar or weigh the water.) Measure also the amount of water the jar holds when it is full. You will find that it is about five times as much.

One-fifth of the air is oxygen and four-fifths nitrogen.

## 6. *When air is heated*

The difficulty of showing the effect of heat on air is that air is invisible. A drop of coloured water may, however, be used to show how far air extends in a tube.

**Experiment 1.** Cork a bottle tightly with a cork having a piece of glass tubing through it. Before pushing in the cork dip the end of the tube in coloured water. When the cork is in place the drop of water should be just clear of the cork.

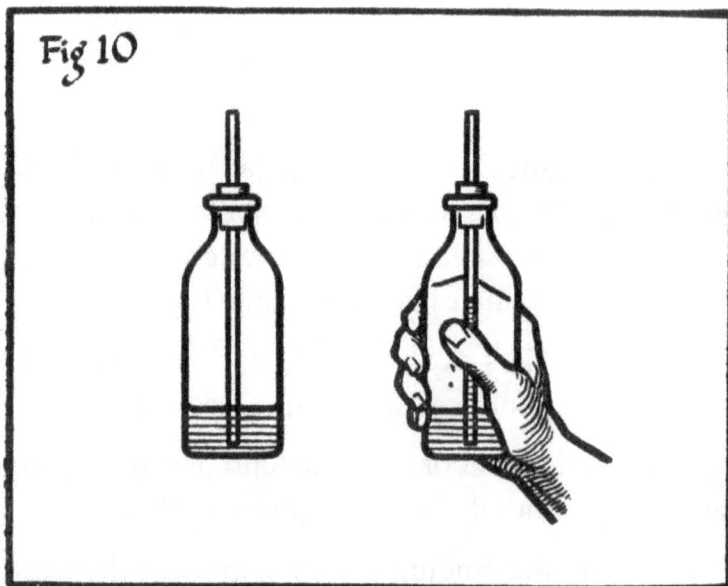

Fig 10

Place the bottle on its side and heat it gently by holding it in the hands. It will be seen that the water moves out, showing that the air in the bottle has expanded.

**Experiment 2.** This is a warm air toy. (Figure 10.)

Get a small bottle which can be held comfortably in the hand. Put some red ink in it and cork it with a cork through which passes a piece of narrow glass tubing. The tubing should reach to the bottom of the bottle. The cork may be waxed to keep it airtight.

Hold the bottle in the hand. The expanding air drives the red ink up the tube. The point is to see how far you can raise it.

**Experiment 3.** Use the same bottle as in Experiment 1. (Figure 11.)

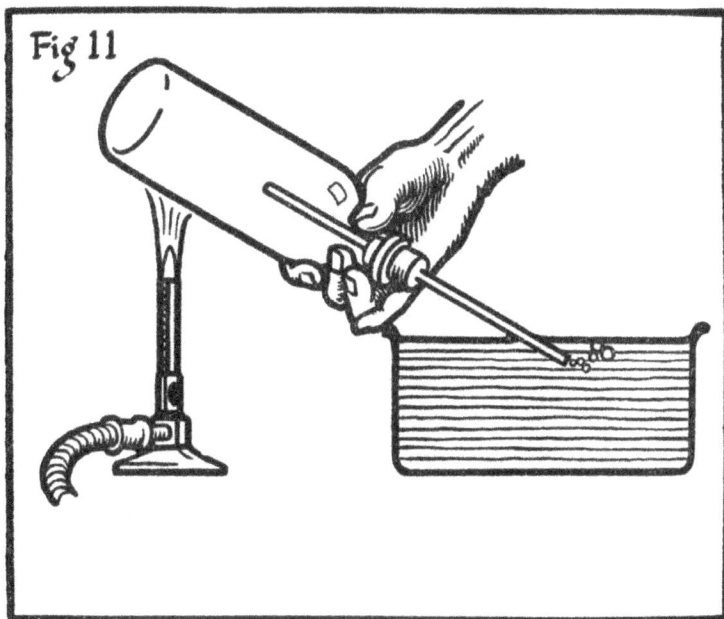

Fig 11

Fix the bottle upright with the end of the tube passing under water in a basin. (The bottle may be held in a retort stand, or tied to a rod across two piles of books, or simply held in the hand.)

Heat the bottle gently by allowing a small gas flame to flicker about it. The expanding air will be seen bubbling through the water.

Leave the bottle to cool. The pressure of the air outside being now greater than that inside, will force water up the tube into the bottle.

*Notes:* i. If you have any difficulty in seeing that hot air is lighter than cold air, think of a bottle of air. When the air is heated it expands and some pours out. There is the same volume of air as before (the bottleful), but there is less weight because some of the air poured out.

ii. It is sometimes said that "hot air rises". This is only true in the sense that any heavy thing rises—when it is pushed up. Hot air is often pushed up by heavier cold air.

**Experiment 4.** Close the door and windows of the room. Hang a thermometer near the ceiling for ten minutes and note the temperature. Find the temperature also near the floor. Usually the temperature is higher near the ceiling. The light warm air is above the heavier cold air.

**Experiment 5.** On a calm day close all the openings in the room except one window. Leave this window open an inch or two at top and bottom. (Figure 12.)

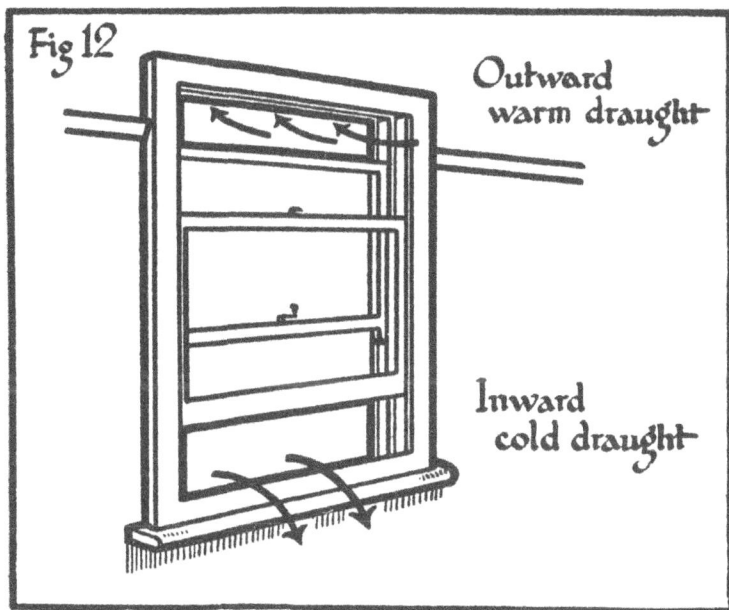

Hold a piece of smouldering paper near each opening in turn. The smoke will show an inward current below and an outward current above.

Windows should be left open above and below for ventilation. The inward current of cool fresh air will drive out the warm stale air above.

**Experiment 6.** Light a candle, place it on the table, and put a lamp chimney over it. If the chimney fits down flat the candle will soon go out.

Light the candle again and put the lamp chimney over it. Just as the candle is going out raise the chimney slightly. The rush of cold air from below drives out the hot used up air and the candle burns up again.

**Experiment 7.** Cut a strip of paper or thin card that will just go into the lamp chimney. (Figure 13.)

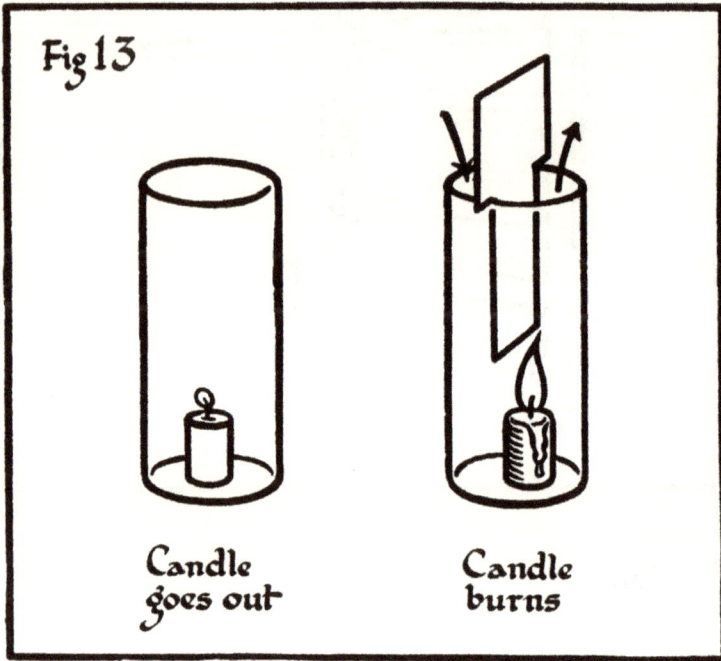

Fig 13

Candle goes out

Candle burns

Light a candle and put the chimney over it. Just as the candle is going out push the paper down into the chimney a little to one side of the candle. The candle will burn up at once.

Hold a piece of smouldering paper above the chimney, first at one side of the paper and then at the other side. The smoke will show that there is a downward current on the side away from the candle, and an upward current above the candle.

(At first all the air above the candle was heated and there was no cold air to drive it up. This is a case where hot air does not rise—because it is not pushed up.)

## *Summary: Science of the Air*

### How we know there is air

Although we cannot see air we know it is all about us because of its effects. For example, water does not enter a bottle unless the air in it is allowed to escape.

Air resists the movement of things through it. The greater the moving surface the greater is the resistance of the air.

### Air pressure

Air pressure on one side of a thing is usually balanced by an equal pressure on the other side, so that the effects are not observed. When the air pressure is not balanced it is seen to be very great. (The pressure of air is about fifteen pounds on every square inch of surface.)

Water is raised in a syringe by decreasing the air pressure inside the syringe whilst the pressure outside remains unchanged.

Water may be moved from one vessel to another at a lower level by siphoning. The air pressures at the ends of the siphon tube balance, but in the longer limb there is a greater length of water pressing down.

Air pressure at any point is the same in all directions.

Air is elastic.

**Things need air to burn**

Things do not burn unless there is a constant supply of air.

In burning, part of the air is used up. This part is called oxygen and forms about one-fifth of the air. The remaining four-fifths is chiefly a gas called nitrogen, in which things do not burn.

**Heated air**

When air is heated it expands. A result of this is that warm air is lighter than cold air.

Rooms are best ventilated by leaving windows open both top and bottom. An inward stream of heavier cold air below drives out the lighter warm air above.

There is a strong draught up chimneys because the hot air in the chimney is forced up by the heavier cold air outside.

# CHAPTER II

# LESSONS ON WATER

### 1. Water

**Experiment 1.** Pour water into various vessels. Notice that when it is still the surface is always flat and level. Hold a glass of water tilted in various directions. The surface is always flat and level.

**Experiment 2.** When water is poured notice that it always flows down.

Use a bent tube (or a piece of rubber tubing) as a siphon to carry water from one vessel to another. The water rises in the siphon tube, but it is forced up by air pressure.

Raise the outside end of the siphon tube slowly. Notice that the water stops running when the end of the tube is above the level of the water. A siphon cannot be used to raise water.

**Experiment 3.** Half fill a bent glass tube with water and fix it upright.

Stand some distance away and hold a ruler at arm's length. Raise the ruler slowly to a level with the water in the tube. Notice that the level is the same in both limbs of the tube.

Repeat the experiment with the tube tilted in various ways.

**Experiment 4.** Use a teapot with the top of the spout on a level with the top of the pot.

Fill the teapot with water. Notice that water begins to flow out of the spout when the pot is full, showing that the level of the water is the same in the pot and the spout.

**Experiment 5.** A small fountain may be made as follows: Have a piece of narrow tubing soldered into the side of a large tin near the bottom. The tubing should be bent up at right angles. (Figure 14.)

Fig 14

Put a finger over the end of the tube and fill the tin with water. Remove the finger and note how the water shoots up.

Note carefully the height to which the water rises. It is very nearly the same as the height of the water in the reservoir (that is, the height to which the water would rise if the tube were carried up higher).

Fountains are fed by a reservoir some height above the level of the openings.

**Experiment 6.** A spring may be imitated in a small box. (Figure 15.)

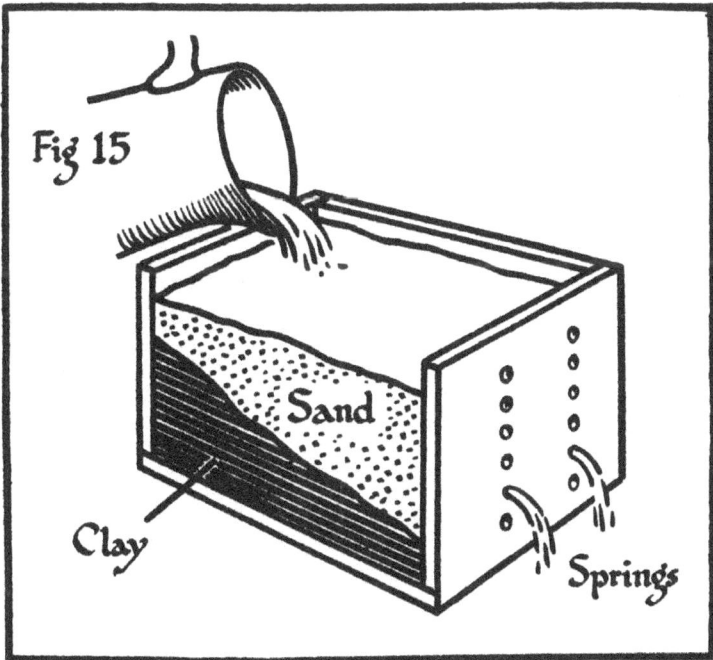

Fig 15
Sand
Clay
Springs

Bore holes in one end of the box with a gimlet. There may be two columns of holes, six holes in each.

Fill the bottom of the box with clay or plasticine, sloping down toward the end with the holes. Fill up the box with sand.

Sprinkle water on the sand to imitate rain. The water will sink through the sand, but not through the clay. It will run down the clay slope and come out as springs at the gimlet holes where the clay ends.

Go on sprinkling water till the springs begin to run. They will then go on running after the sprinkling has stopped.

**Experiment 7.** Shake up a little salt with water in a bottle. Notice that the salt dissolves.

Find other things which dissolve in water. Test sugar, soda, sulphur, powdered chalk, charcoal, and any other things you can think of. Powder the stuff in each case and only use a little.

**Experiment 8.** Cut out a circle of blotting-paper. Fold it in two and then in two again. Open it out so as to make a cone. (There will be three thicknesses at one side and one at the other.) (Figure 16.)

Place the filter-paper in the mouth of a small jar. Pour a little water into it. You will see that the water runs through into the jar.

Shake up a little earth in a bottle of water to make it muddy. Pour some of the muddy water into the filter-paper. You will see that clear water runs through the filter-paper. The mud is left behind on the filter-paper.

If the water which comes through is not quite clear, filter it again through another filter-paper.

# Fig 16

1

2

3

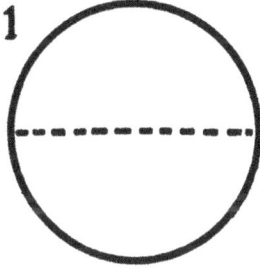

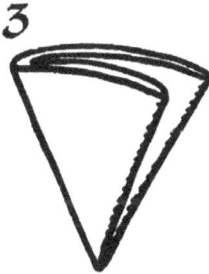

5 Ready for use

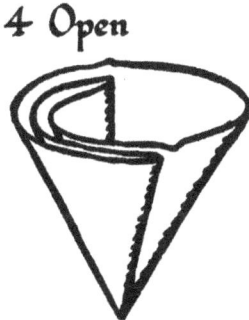

4 Open

## 2. Solutions

**Experiment 1.** Shake up a little sand and a little salt separately with water. Notice that the salt dissolves, but not the sand.

Make a mixture of sand and salt. Taste a little of the mixture and notice the salt taste.

The sand may be freed from salt. Put the mixture in a jar and fill up with water. Stir, and then leave to settle. Taste the liquid and notice the salt taste.

Pour off the salt solution. Fill up with water again, stir, and leave to settle. The water this time is hardly salt at all.

After several washings there will be hardly a trace of salt in the sand. Taste the sand to see if there is any salt with it.

The sand may be spread out and left to dry or it may be dried quickly on a large tin lid over a gas flame.

**Experiment 2.** Take some of the first salt solution obtained by washing the sand. Filter the solution if it is not clear.

Pour some of the solution into a large tin lid and leave it to dry up in the sun. Taste the white solid left behind to see if it is salt.

Another lot of salt solution may be dried up rapidly over a gas flame.

**Experiment 3.** Fill a small bottle half full of water. Put in some salt and shake it up. If all the salt dissolves, add more, and shake up again. Go on adding salt a little at a time. A point is soon reached when no more salt dissolves. The solution is then said to be saturated.

Add a little salt to a saturated solution. Notice that it still remains after much shaking.

**Experiment 4.** Fill two small bottles half full of water. Choose two lumps of sugar about the same size. Powder one lump.

Put the whole lump in one bottle (or break the lump if it will not go in whole) and the powdered lump in the other bottle. Shake up the two bottles at the same time. You will find that the powdered sugar dissolves more quickly than the other. This is because there is a bigger surface for the water to touch.

**Experiment 5.** Put a lump of sugar in a cup of hot water and another in a cup of cold water. Stir the two at the same time. You will find that the sugar dissolves much more quickly in the hot water than in the cold.

**Experiment 6.** Make a cold saturated solution of sugar in a small bottle. Add a little more sugar. Heat the water very gently over a gas flame. The sugar will dissolve in the warm water.

Make the water hot and you will find that much more sugar will dissolve in it.

**Experiment 7.** Make a strong solution of saltpetre in hot water. Leave the solution to cool.

As the solution cools you will see some of the saltpetre reappear as small crystals. The liquid left is a saturated solution of saltpetre.

**Experiment 8.** Crush some washing soda, dissolve it in water, and notice the soapy feel of the solution.

**Experiment 9.** Pour some tap water into a large tin lid. Leave it in the sun to dry up. (It would be better to heat it over a gas flame.)

When the tin is dry look and see if there is any solid left. If there is not much, fill up the tin again and let the water evaporate once more.

There is always some solid matter dissolved in tap water.

### 3. Crystals

**Experiment 1.** Dissolve some powdered saltpetre in warm water in a small bottle. Shake up more saltpetre till no more will dissolve. Then leave the water to cool.

As the water cools small crystals form. Pour them out on a piece of blotting-paper. It will be seen that they are not a powder but small shapes.

**Experiment 2.** i. Dissolve as much saltpetre as will dissolve in warm water (not much more than lukewarm). Leave it to cool.

ii. Dissolve as much saltpetre as will dissolve in hot water. Cool the water quickly by holding the bottle in which it is contained in cold water.

iii. Examine the two lots of crystals. It will be seen that larger crystals are formed when the water cools slowly.

**Experiment 3.** Still larger crystals may be formed by making a solution of saltpetre in cold water and leaving the solution in a bottle to evaporate slowly.

When a few crystals have formed, take them out, choose the best of them, and put one or two of these back.

Grow large crystals in this way also of alum, and any other salts that are available.

**Experiment 4.** Examine crystals with a magnifying glass. Make a note of the shape and any other points: c.g.

Common salt crystals are little white cubes.

Saltpetre crystals are needle-shaped, and colourless.

Borax crystals are prisms. They have a greasy lustre.

Copper sulphate crystals are transparent blue slabs.

**Experiment 5.** Some crystals contain water— "water of crystallization". This water may be driven off by heating the crystals.

i. Put a few crystals of washing soda on a tin lid and heat them over a gas flame. It will be seen that water boils away and a white powder (not crystals) is left. Hold a cold plate or slate over the crystals while they are being heated. Some of the water will condense on it.

ii. Leave a clear crystal of washing soda exposed to the air for some days. Watch it day by day. It will gradually become covered with white powder as it loses its water of crystallization.

iii. Heat some salt gently on a tin lid. It will be seen that no water is given off:

iv. Test any other salts in the same way. Copper sulphate is interesting. The large blue crystals change to a white powder when the water is driven off. Add a little water to this white powder and it turns blue again.

**Experiment 6.** Make a hot strong solution of sugar. Dip some pieces of thin string in the solution and leave it to cool. Sugar crystals will form along the strings as the solution cools.

**Experiment 7.** Put some sulphur in a deep tin lid. Heat it very gently over a small gas flame. When the sulphur is melted leave it to cool.

As soon as a crust forms on the surface of the melted sulphur, take up the tin lid with a cloth holder and pour out the liquid sulphur. Pointed sulphur crystals will be seen where some of the sulphur has become solid.

**Experiment 8.** Examine a piece of granite with a magnifying glass. You will see that it is made up of a large number of crystals mixed together. You may be able to distinguish colourless hexagonal prisms of quartz, reddish crystals of felspar, and flat plates of mica.

### 4. When water is heated

When heating a jar of water over a gas flame place a piece of wire gauze between the flame and the jar. Unless a flask is used keep the flame small.

**Experiment 1.** Get a jar with a narrow neck and a cork to fit it. Pass a piece of glass tubing through the cork. Let it stick out about an inch below the cork.

Fill the jar with water and cork it. See that there is no air below the cork.

i. Heat the jar gently. Notice the bubbles which begin to rise. These bubbles collect round the tube below the cork. You can see that these bubbles are not steam because steam would not collect in water only rather warm. They are air that was dissolved in the water. Note that heated water cannot contain so much dissolved air as cold water.

ii. Remove the cork and heat the jar more strongly. After a time bubbles of steam begin to form at the bottom. Notice how they become larger, break away, and rise to the surface.

After a time there is a quick and steady stream of steam bubbles from all parts of the water. The water is now boiling.

iii. Use a thick duster to take the jar from the flame, pour out a little water, and put the cork and tube back again. Go on heating the water.

You can see that the steam which comes out of the tube is invisible. Where it reaches the cold air it changes to a cloud. This cloud disappears as it rises. It changes to vapour again.

Hold a plate or other cold surface in the stream of steam. The cold surface changes the steam back to water.

**Experiment 2.** Use the same jar as in Experiment 1, but use a longer piece of glass tubing. (Figure 17.)

Fill the jar with coloured water. Push the tube into the cork till the end of it is just level with the bottom of the cork. Fix the cork tightly in the bottle. Push in the tube a little further.

It is convenient to have a scale. Cut two slits in a slip of paper, mark a scale on this (inches and tenths of an inch will do), and put the tube through the slits.

Heat the jar gently and watch the coloured water.

At first the water falls a little. This is because the glass is heated first. It expands and leaves more room in the jar.

Afterwards the water steadily rises, showing that water expands when it is heated.

Remove the gas flame. At first the water rises quickly in the tube. This is because the glass jar cools first, contracts, and squeezes out some of the water.

Afterwards the coloured water falls slowly till it is nearly at its first level.

**Experiment 3.** Fill a wide-mouthed jar with water. Put some sawdust in the water. (A few crystals of permanganate of potash will do instead of the sawdust.)

Heat the water very gently near the middle of the jar. The sawdust shows the movements of the water. The more heated water at the middle is lighter than the colder water at the sides and is pushed up by the heavier water. There is an upward stream of warmer

Fig 17

water in the middle, and a downward stream of cooler water all round.  (Figure 18.)

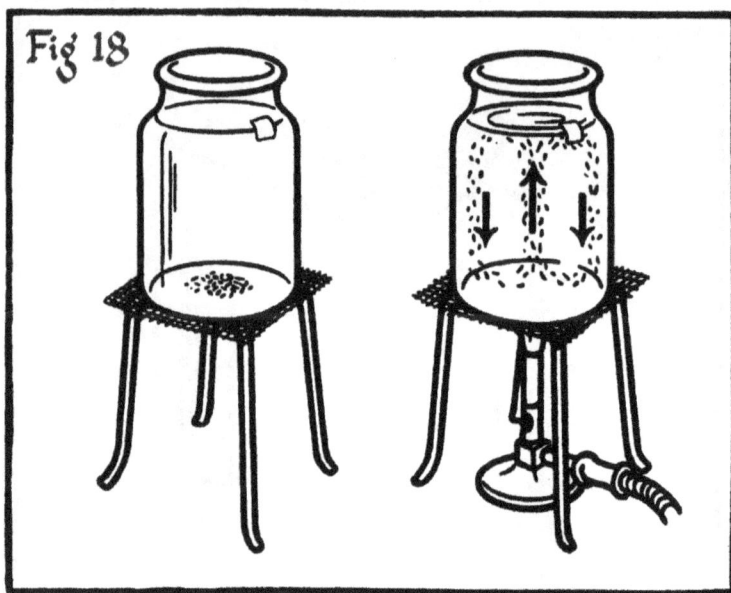

Fill the jar with fresh water and sawdust, and repeat the experiment with a small gas flame close to the outside rim of the jar.

If a small tank is available it would be interesting to repeat this experiment on a larger scale.

It may be noted that ocean currents are convection currents of this kind between the heated water near the equator and the cold water nearer the poles.

### 5.  *When water dries up*

**Experiment 1.**  Leave a saucer of water exposed to the air and examine it day by day.  Notice that the water gradually dries up.

**Experiment 2.** Place equal amounts of water in a saucer and in a tumbler and leave them side by side for some days. Water dries up more quickly from the saucer, where the surface is greater.

The surface can be further increased by leaving sheets of blotting-paper dipping into the water. The rate at which the water dries up will be much increased.

**Experiment 3.** Dip two similar sheets of blotting-paper in water. Hang them up, one in warm sunshine, and the other in a cooler place. It will be found that the warm sheet dries up quickest.

Test also two damp sheets of blotting-paper, one hung up in a draught and the other in a place free from draught. It will be found that the draught increases the rate of drying up.

**Experiment 4.** Write with ink on two pieces of paper. Leave one on the desk and wave the other about. The latter dries up quicker. Waving it about has the same effect as placing it in a draught. In each case fresh air is continually reaching the moisture.

**Experiment 5.** Try this experiment on a hot day.

Fill two similar bottles with water. Cover each with flannel. Leave one dry and dip the other in water. Hang the two bottles up in a draught (or simply let them stand on a table).

When the damp flannel dries, moisten it again. Taste the water from each bottle at the end of a hot dry afternoon. It will be found that the bottle with a damp covering is much colder. In drying up the water takes heat from the bottle and the water in the bottle.

In the same way the drying up of sweat cools the skin.

Unglazed jars are used in hot countries to keep drinking-water cool. A little water soaks through the jar, dries up, and so cools the remaining water.

**Experiment 6.** A butter-cooler may be made from strips of wood. (Figure 19.)

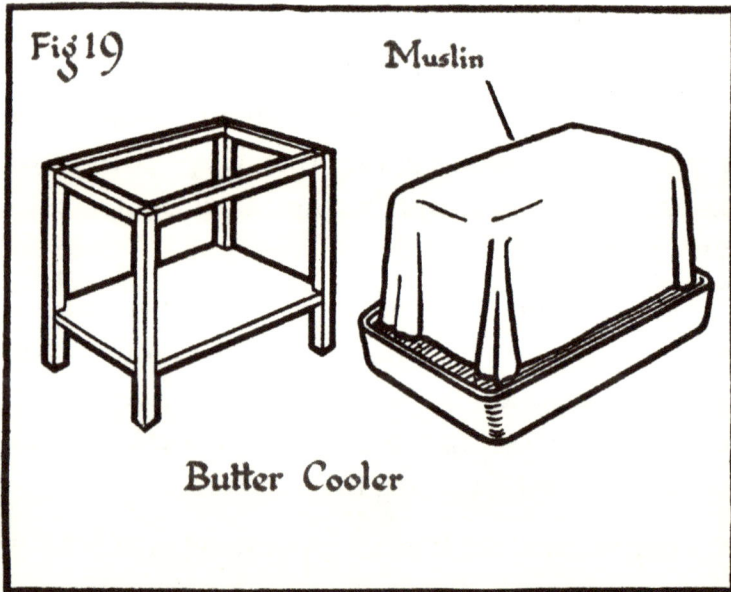

Fig 19

Muslin

Butter Cooler

Make the strips into an open box with four legs. Let the box stand in a basin of water and cover it with muslin dipping into the water all round.

It will be found that water soaks up into the muslin, dries up, and so keeps the box cool.

Place a piece of butter in the butter-cooler on a hot day, and compare it with a piece left in a similar position away from the butter-cooler.

**Experiment 7.** There is always some moisture in the air.

Bring a glass of freshly drawn cold water into the room. There is usually moisture on the cold surface of the glass. If ice is added to the water the amount of moisture which forms on the glass is increased.

After a short time the moisture dries up again.

**Experiment 8.** Some kinds of stuff take moisture from the air. One of these is calcium chloride which is used as a disinfectant. Unless kept in a well-corked bottle it quickly becomes damp. It can be dried by heating it.

Place some dry calcium chloride on a saucer and leave it exposed to the air. Examine it several times during the day. You will find that it becomes more and more damp.

In a day or two the calcium chloride will have taken so much moisture from the air that it dissolves in the water it has collected.

It may be noted that when the air is sufficiently cooled water vapour condenses to water and falls as rain.

## 6. *Water pressure*

**Experiment 1.** Weigh out a pound of water. Place a jar on one scale-pan. On the other pan put books or other objects to balance it. When it is balanced add a one-pound weight. Pour water into the jar till the pound weight is balanced.

**Experiment 2.** Find the weight of a cubic foot of water.

Counterpoise a jar. Pour into it a measured quantity of water from a measuring jar. Add weights to balance the weight of this water. Find the weight of one cubic inch, and from this the weight of 1728 cubic inches. (It would be convenient to find the weight of 72 cubic inches in a three-pound jam jar, and then to multiply by 24.)

**Experiment 3.** Water presses in other directions besides downward.

Place a cork or a piece of wood at the bottom of a jar. Pour in some water. The cork is pressed upward.

**Experiment 4.** Cut a piece of cardboard that will fit over the end of a lamp chimney with a little to spare. (A thin flat piece of tin is better.) (Figure 20.)

Place the card over the end of the chimney, hold it there, and lower that end into a basin of water. When you let go the card it is held up by the pressure of the water.

Carefully pour water into the chimney. When the

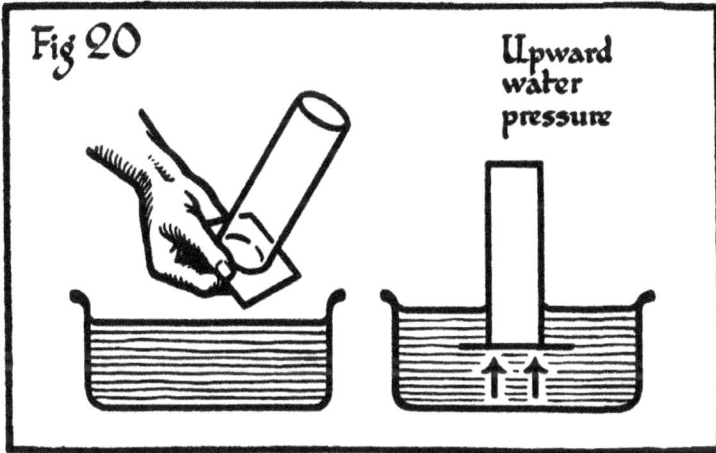

level of the water inside is equal to that outside, the card will float away. The downward pressure of the water in the chimney just balances the upward pressure of the water outside.

**Experiment 5.** Get a small tin (a cigarette tin will do). Make two nail-holes close together, but one in the side and one in the bottom.

Cover the holes with the fingers, hold the tin over a basin, and fill it with water.

Open the hole in the bottom. Water rushes straight down. Tilt the tin various ways. You should be able to see that the water begins to rush out at right angles to the bottom of the tin.

Use the hole in the side in the same way.

**Experiment 6.** Use the same tin as for Experiment 5. If it is filled with water, the water at once begins to run out through both holes. If the downward pressure of the water were greater than the sideways pressure we should expect more water to run out through the hole in the bottom.  (Figure 21.)

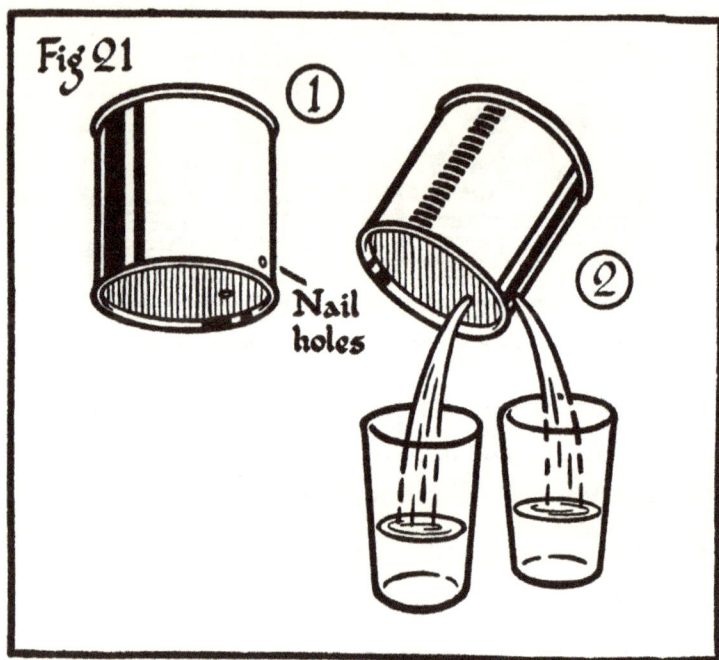

Fig 21

① Nail holes ②

Place two tumblers on the table.  Hold the tin above them so that the water from one hole will flow into each.  Cover the holes, fill the tin with water, and then open the holes.

When the tin is empty examine the water in the tumblers.  It will be found that there is the same amount in each, showing that the sideways pressure is equal to the downward pressure.

The experiment may be repeated with the tin tilted in various ways to show that the pressure of the water is the same in all directions.

**Experiment 7.** Get a long tin can (such as those used to hold lawn sand). Make five nail-holes in a line down the side, the top one being about a quarter of the way down. (Figure 22.)

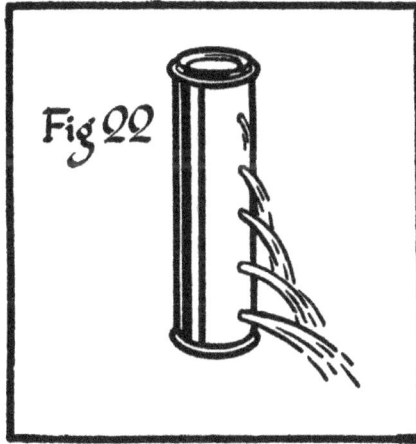

Place the tin in a basin, cover the holes with the fingers, and fill the tin with water. Open the holes. It will be seen that the water shoots out most strongly through the bottom hole, less strongly through the next above, and so on. This shows that the pressure increases with depth.

Keep the tin filled by pouring in water from a jug. Collect in tumblers the water from two of the holes. The amount of water collected will give a rough measure of the pressures. It will be found that if the depth (from the surface) is twice as great at one point as at another, the pressure is twice as great, if the depth is three times as great, the pressure is three times as great, and so on.

Note also that at a depth of one foot the pressure on one square foot is the weight of a cubic foot of water (62 ½ lb.).

## 7. *Floating things*

*Note:* A spring balance is a cheap and convenient weighing machine. It is well to have at least two, one weighing up to a pound, and the other to at least seven pounds.

**Experiment 1.** Hang a stone by means of string from the hook of a spring balance. Note the weight of the stone.

Hold the balance over a jar of water, and lower it till the stone is under water, but not touching the sides or the bottom of the jar.

Watch the indicator on the balance. The weight shown is less and less as the stone sinks into the water. When the stone is all under water the indicator remains steady again. Note that part of the weight of the stone is supported by the upward pressure of the water on the stone. Find how much is supported.

**Experiment 2.** Find how much water is displaced by the stone. Half fill a measuring jar with water. Note the level. Put the stone in the jar (it should be all under water). Note the level again and find the volume of water displaced.

Another way is to use a jar or jug with a spout. Fill

the jar with water till it is just about to pour over. Then lower the stone gently into the water and collect the water that flows over in a small weighed jar. Weigh the jar again to find the weight of water displaced by the stone. (Figure 23.)

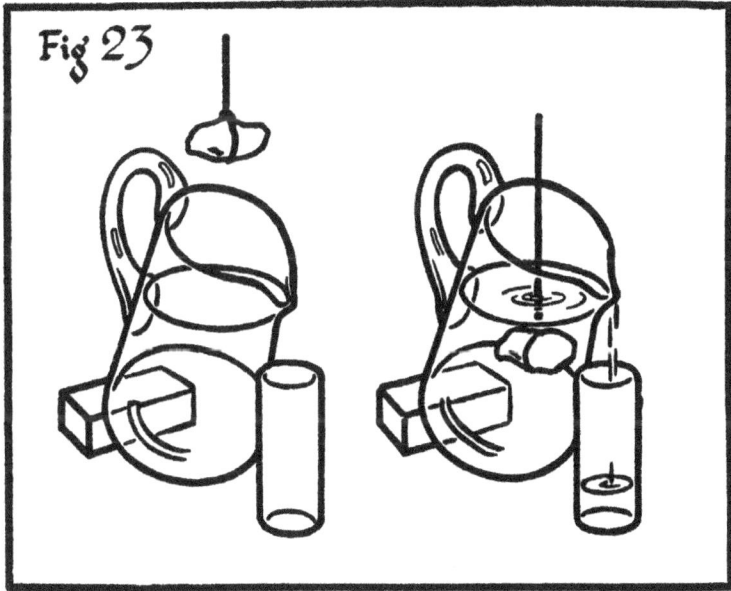

Fig 23

**Experiment 3.** Find:

i. The upward push of water on a stone.

ii. The weight of water displaced by the stone

Careful work will show that the two are equal. Your results will probably be not quite equal because the methods of weighing are not quite accurate.

Test other things—other stones, pieces of iron, lead, brass, etc.

**Experiment 4.** Find the weight of water displaced by a floating cork.

Weigh the cork. You will find that the two weights are equal.

Test other floating things. In every case the upward push of the water is equal to the weight of the object.

Push the cork under water with a knitting needle, and find the weight of water displaced by it when it is completely under water. This weight is greater than the weight of the cork.

The water pushes the cork up till some of it is above the surface of the water. The upward push of the water and the weight of the cork then just balance.

Test other floating things in the same way.

**Experiment 5.** Fill a small tin (a cigarette tin will do) with water and place it in a basin of water. It sinks.

Now empty the tin. It floats. To make it float upright put in it small pieces of lead or pebbles.

To show why the empty tin floats: Fill the jar or jug with a spout with water. Place the tin in it and catch the displaced water in a small weighed jar. Weigh the displaced water and note that it is equal to the weight of the tin.

Now add small weights to the tin till it is just about to sink. At this point weigh the tin and the displaced water again. They are still equal.

If further weights are added to the tin the weight of

the tin is greater than that of the displaced water and the tin sinks.

An iron ship floats because its weight is less than the weight of water it displaces when just about to sink. If it were pressed down nearly to the water line the water would push it up again.

**Experiment 6.** Weight a toy wooden brick at one end so that it floats upright. Float it in a jar of water and mark the depth to which it sinks.

Fill the jar with strong salt solution and find the depth to which the wooden brick sinks in this. You will find that it does not sink so deep.

To find the reason fill the jar with a spout with the salt solution. Put the wooden brick in it, and find the weight of salt solution displaced. You will find that it is equal to the weight of the brick.

The salt solution is heavier than water so that a less volume of it is displaced by the wooden brick.

When a ship sails from a river to the sea it floats a little higher when it reaches the salt sea water.

**Experiment 7.** To show that salt solution is heavier than water:

Weigh a bottle, fill it with water, weigh again, and find the weight of the water.

Pour out the water, fill the bottle with salt solution, weigh, and find the weight of the salt solution.

**Experiment 8.** Put a fresh egg in a tall jar half full of water. The egg sinks. (Figure 24.)

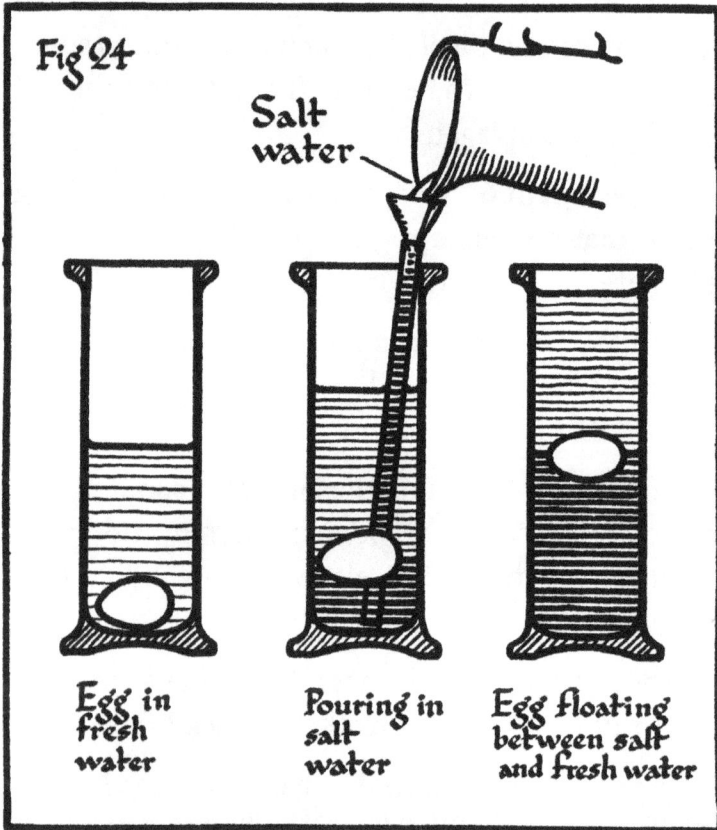

Fig 24

Salt water

Egg in fresh water

Pouring in salt water

Egg floating between salt and fresh water

Make some strong salt solution and colour it with red ink.

Make a paper tube that will reach to the bottom of the jar. Pour salt solution down the tube. The egg will float up on the salt solution and you can have it floating half way up the jar.

## 8. The elastic skin of water

**Experiment 1.** Look at the hairs of a dry paint brush. You will see that they stand apart. Dip the brush in water. The hairs still stand apart. Lift the brush out of the water. The hairs cling together in a wet mass. The surface of the water holds them together as if it were a thin sheet of elastic. (Figure 25.)

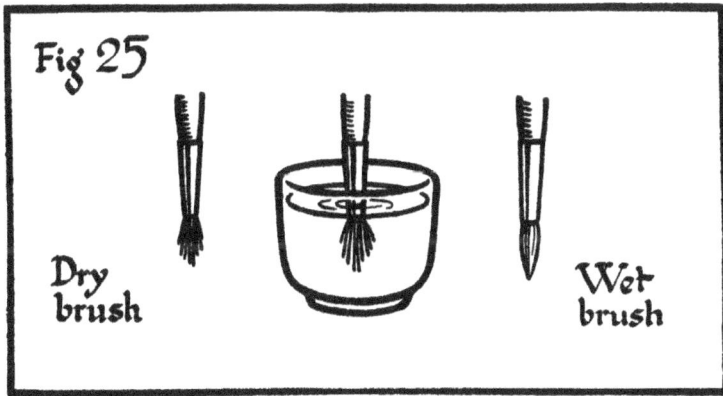

Fig 25  Dry brush  Wet brush

**Experiment 2.** Turn on a tap so that it drips very slowly, or place a loosely corked bottle of water on its side so that it drips slowly. Watch the water dripping.

The water collects until the weight of the drop is great enough to break through the surface of the water. You may be able to see that the drops are all about the same size. The same weight is required in each case to break through the water surface.

**Experiment 3.** Place a sewing needle carefully on the surface of water in a basin. The needle floats, but at a touch it breaks through the surface and sinks. If you have any difficulty in placing things on the surface of water, rub them with vaseline or other grease and hold them flat.

A flat strip of tin, a safety razor blade, a fret saw, and other small objects may be supported on the surface of water. In each case the object sinks as soon as it is wetted, that is when it breaks through the water surface.

You will find that a wet needle does not float.

Look out on ponds and rivers for the small animals which run about the surface of the water without breaking through. If one of these animals is wetted it sinks through the surface into the water, and it has difficulty in breaking through the water surface from below.

**Experiment 4.** It is possible to float a sieve on the surface of water. (Figure 26.)

Fig 26

Make the sieve out of thin wire gauze. Cut a circle of wire gauze about six inches across. Bend the gauze up all round to form a sieve. Grease the wires slightly but see that the holes are left open, otherwise it ceases to be a sieve.

Place the sieve lightly on water in a basin. The water does not come through the narrow holes in the sieve. Masts and sails for the floating sieve may be made from thin strips of wood and paper. The sieve will carry small toy animals.

The wire gauze may also be flattened out and used as a raft.

Notice that the sieve does not float as a piece of wood floats or as a ship floats. It is on the surface of the water. Wet the wires of the sieve by brushing them with a wet brush. Water begins to run in and the sieve sinks.

**Experiment 5.** Use the same sieve as in the last experiment. See that it is quite dry. Put a piece of thin paper in the bottom of the sieve and then pour in a little water. The paper may now be removed and the sieve will hold the water.

The under surface of the water across the small holes is not broken through by the water above.

**Experiment 6.** Pour water into a bottle with a narrow neck. You will find that the air in the bottle prevents the water going in easily. Unless you are careful the water will splash all round. (Figure 27.)

Fig 27

Now place a thin rod in the bottle and pour water down the rod. The surface of the water holds the water to the rod and it runs down the rod into the bottle.

**Experiment 7.** Pour water along a sloping rod. If you pour gently the water will run for some distance along the rod. It is held to the rod by the surface.

Get a piece of thick string and wet it thoroughly. Fix it up slanting with the lower end dipping into a jar. Pour water very gently on the upper end of the string. The surface of the water will hold it to the string and the water will run down into the jar.

## 9. *The skin of other liquids*

**Experiment 1.** Place side by side a saucer full of water and another full of soap solution (shake up soft soap with water). Float a flat piece of tin on the water. Then try and float it on the soap solution. You will find that it floats more readily on the water.

Experiment with a safety razor blade. It will float on water with quite a third of its surface under the water. Even if it floats at all on soap solution the least touch sends it under.

The surface of the soap solution will bear less heavy weights than the surface of water. This is why soap solution may be used to clear plants of green fly. The flies sink through the surface and are drowned.

**Experiment 2.** Fill a basin with clean water. Float a dozen matches or thin strips of wood in a circle with their ends close together. (Figure 28.)

Fig 28

Touch the water at the centre with a strip of soap. The matches at once move away from the soap. This is because the pull of the water surface is greater than the pull of the soapy surface at the centre.

**Experiment 3.** Fill a basin with clean water. Notice that the surface is clear and bright. Let a drop of oil fall on the surface. You will see the oily patch gradually grow bigger and bigger. The surface pull of the water is greater than that of the oil, and so the oil is pulled out.

After a time you may see colours on the surface of the water. These colours show that the oil has been drawn out very thin over the water.

**Experiment 4.** Make a spiral of thin wire. Float it on water in a basin. There may be a little difficulty in getting the spiral flat enough to float. Flatten it bit by bit with the fingers. (Figure 29.)

Fig 29

Take a spoonful of soap solution. Let a drop or two fall in the centre of the spiral. As the soap solution is drawn out along the spiral by the greater pull of the water surface, the spiral will slowly spin round so that the outside point is moving forward. (If this is bent down slightly it will break through the water surface and the spiral will sink.)

Notice that the spiral is pushed round by the soap solution surface which is itself drawn out by the greater water surface pull.

**Experiment 5.** Cut out a torpedo shape in thin cardboard. Cut a narrow channel from the tail to the middle. (Figure 30.)

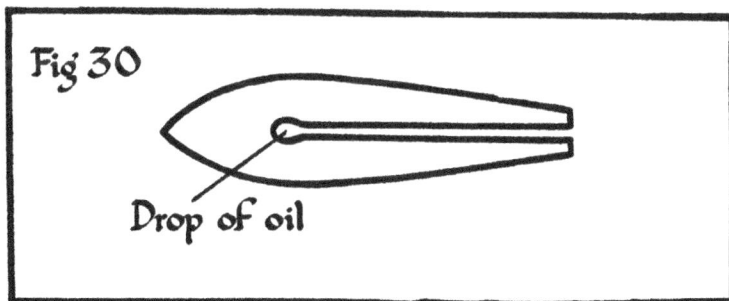

Fig 30

Drop of oil

Float the torpedo in water and drop a little oil at the inner end of the channel. As the oil spreads out the torpedo will be driven along.

The torpedo may also be driven by a drop or two of soap solution.

**Experiment 6.** The behaviour of camphor in water is quite amusing provided the water is free from grease. If there is any grease the camphor will only move feebly or not at all.

Wash a basin well with soda and rinse with clean tap-water. Then fill the basin with clean water.

Drop a few tiny scraps of camphor on the water. They will be seen to dart about in a most lively manner. The camphor dissolves unevenly. Where it dissolves it weakens the surface pull of the water at that point, and the camphor is at once drawn away from it.

**Experiment 7.** Wash a basin well with soda, rinse with clean tap-water, and fill the basin with clean water

Make a tiny boat of thin tin. (The inside cover of cigarette tins is suitable.) A match stalk and a scrap of paper may be gummed in place for mast and sails.

Place a piece of camphor at the back of the boat where it can touch the water. Then put the little boat on the water in the basin. (Figure 31.)

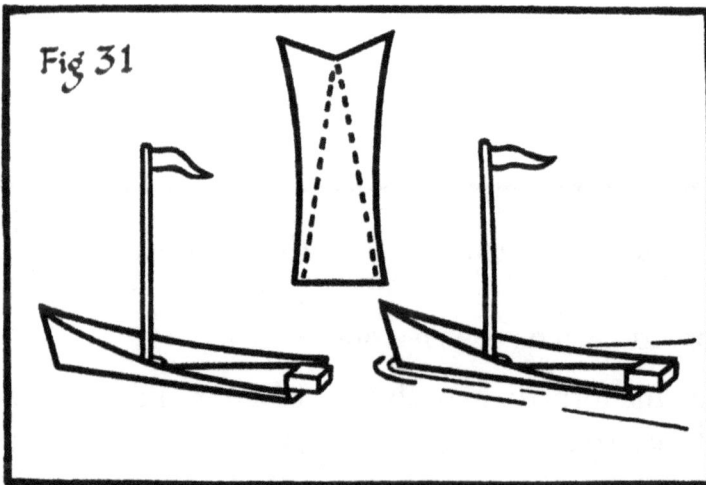

Fig 31

The camphor dissolves and weakens the surface pull behind, so that the boat is drawn along by the greater pull of pure water in front.

**Experiment 8.** Wash a basin well with soda, rinse with clean tap-water, and fill the basin with clean water.

Cut a piece off a clean cork and push two needles through it from side to side. (The needles should cross at right angles.) (Figure 32.)

Fig 32

Cork

Cut four flat pieces of cork and tie a piece of camphor to one face of each with thin thread. Fix these on the ends of the needles—upright, and with all the four pieces of camphor facing in the same direction.

Copy the dancers and cut them out in thin card. Fix them upright in a slit in the cork.

Place the dancers on the water. They will spin round away from the sides where the dissolving camphor is weakening the surface pull of the water.

If the water is quite clean the dancers will go on spinning round for a long time.

## 10. *Water in narrow tubes*

**Experiment 1.** i. Half fill a glass tumbler with water. Look at the surface of the water, especially where it touches the glass. You will see that it curves up where it touches the glass.

Drop a small toy wooden brick into the water. The water curves up where it touches the brick.

ii. Grease the inside of another tumbler with vaseline. Fill it half full of water. You will find that the water does not wet the greasy tumbler and that the surface curves down where it touches the greased glass.

Grease a small wooden brick and put it in the tumbler. You will see that the water curves down where it touches the greased surface.

**Experiment 2.** Fill a tumbler with water exactly to the brim.

Drop a penny carefully into the water, then another, and another. See how many pennies you can drop in before any water pours over the edge.

Bring your eye to a level with the rim of the glass. You will see that the water is piled up above it, held in by the elastic surface.

Break the surface with your finger at the edge. Water at once begins to pour over.

**Experiment 3.** You can see the curved surface of water much more clearly in a narrow tube.

Hold a piece of narrow glass tubing upright in water. You should notice two things—the surface of the water curves upward where it touches the glass, and the level of the water in the tube is higher than the level of the water outside.

**Experiment 4.** Hold several lengths of glass tubing of different widths, side by side, in coloured water.

Notice the height of the water in the tubes. The narrower the tube the higher the water rises in it.

**Experiment 5.** Place two sheets of glass (clean two photographic plates) so that they touch along one edge of each and are slightly apart along the opposite edges. In this position hold them upright in water.

You will see the water rising in the narrow space. There is a line curving upward from the wide end toward the end where the sheets of glass touch.

**Experiment 6.** Some things are full of small holes and spaces. Water quickly rises into these. To show this use water tinted with red or black ink.

i. Put a lump of sugar in a teaspoon full of tinted water. The water quickly rises through the sugar.

ii. Put the end of a short length of lampwick in a saucer of tinted water. Note that oil rises through the spaces in lampwick just as the tinted water does.

iii. Put a dry sponge in a saucer of tinted water. The whole of the water may rise into the sponge.

iv. Fix a piece of blotting-paper upright in a saucer of tinted water.

v. Fix a piece of cane upright in tinted water. After a little time cut the cane down the middle and notice how the water has risen into it. Note that sap rises in the stems of plants in this way. Cut the stems of several flowers and notice the narrow tubes running along them.

**Experiment 7.** Nearly fill a cup or a jar with water. Place a piece of lampwick with one end in the water and the other end hanging over the side. (Thick string will do but it should first be soaked in water.)

Water will rise up into the wick and after a time it will be seen dripping from the end.

A damp garment will act in the same way if it is left hanging over the side of a basin of water.

**Experiment 8.** Drive a screw into a piece of wood and leave it exposed to the weather for some time. You will then find it difficult to get it out.

Put a little oil round the head of the screw. The oil will soak into the narrow space between the screw and the wood. The screw may then be taken out with a screw-driver.

## 11. Soap bubbles

**Soap solutions.** i. Soft soap shaken up with rain water gives a good soap solution. The addition of a little glycerine improves it.

ii. Castile soap (get this from a chemist) and filtered rain water give a better solution. Again add a little glycerine.

**Experiment 1.** Pour some soap solution into a saucer and practise blowing bubbles with a pipe.

Blow a large bubble. Drain away the drop of liquid below by touching it with a small rod dipped in the soap solution. Raise the pipe quickly and let the bubble float away. The bubble rises because the air in it is warmer than the air outside. The heavier colder air pushes it up. It soon, however, cools and falls.

**Experiment 2.** Light a candle and place it on the table. (Figure 33.)

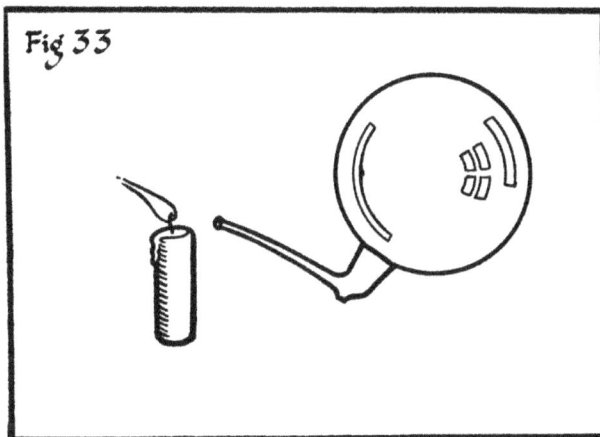

Fig 33

Blow a large bubble and drain away the liquid. Hold the opening in the pipe-stem near the candle flame. The flame will be blown out as the contracting bubble pushes air out of the pipe.

**Experiment 3.** Blow hard into a bubble.Notice how the bubble is pushed out where the stream of air strikes it.

Cover the opening in the stem with a finger. The bubble is seen to be spherical, showing that the air pressure inside is the same in all directions.

**Experiment 4.** Make a ring of wire with part of the wire for a handle. Dip the ring in soap solution. It will come out with a film across it. (Figure 34.)

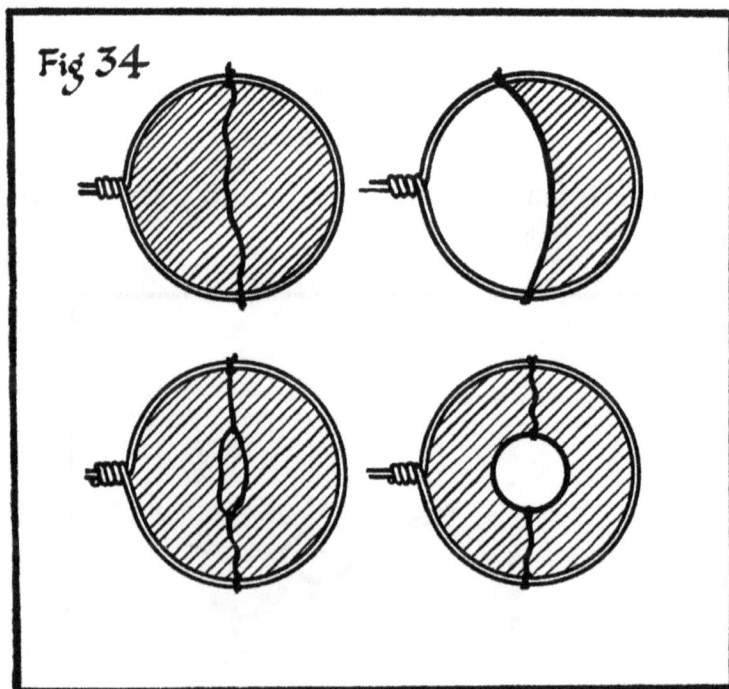

Fig 34

i. Tie a piece of thin thread loosely across the ring. Dip the ring in soap solution and bring it out with a film. Touch the film on one side of the thread to break it. The film on the other side of the thread at once draws the thread into part of a circle curving in toward the film. This is the shape that makes the film as small as possible. Being elastic it has contracted as much as possible.

Make a small loop in the middle of a piece of thread. Tie the thread across the wire ring with the loop in the middle.

Dip the ring in soap solution to make a film. Touch the film inside the loop to break it there. The remainder of the film at once draws the loop of thread out into a circle. The circle is the greatest possible shape that can be made from the loop of thread, so that the remainder of the elastic film has contracted as much as possible.

**Experiment 5.** Fix a wire ring to a small upright stand (a wooden rod nailed to a wooden base).

Dip the ring in soap solution. Blow a bubble wider than the ring, drain away the liquid, let the bubble rest on the ring, and take away the pipe.

The elastic bubble may be pushed through the ring by pressing it gently with the bowl of the pipe.

**Experiment 6.** Blow a soap bubble and place it on the ring wetted with soap solution. (Figure 35.)

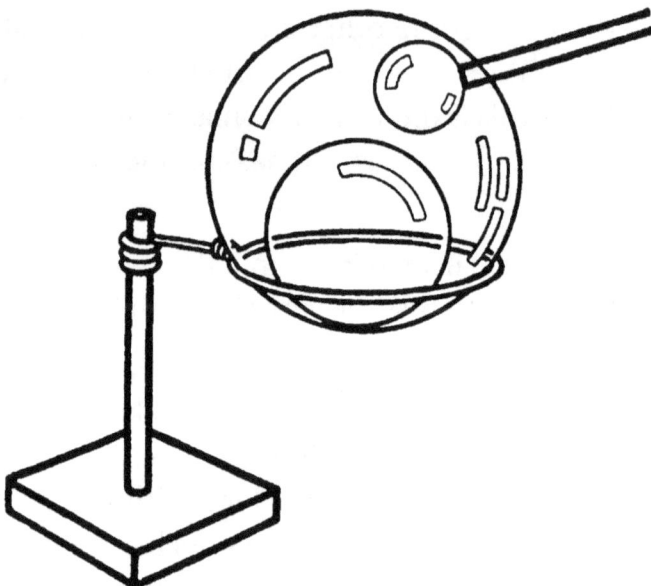

Dip a piece of narrow glass tubing in soap solution. Push the end gently through the first bubble and blow a second bubble inside. With care the tube may be drawn out and the second bubble left resting on the inside of the first.

A third bubble may be blown inside the first or inside the second.

Notice that the bubbles remain separate. Although they appear to be touching there is really a thin film of air between them.

**Experiment 7.** Spread out a silk handkerchief on the table. Soap bubbles may be dropped on this without breaking.

Drop a bubble on the handkerchief.

Rub a fountain pen on the coat sleeve to electrify it. Bring the pen slowly down over the bubble. The bubble will be attracted by the electrified pen.

Several pupils may blow bubbles and let them fall on the handkerchief while another raises them with the electrified pen.

## *Summary: Science of Water*

**Properties of water**

The surface of water at rest is always flat.

Moving water flows down unless it is forced up.

Water in connected vessels rises to the same level in each. In a fountain the water rises nearly to the level of the water in the reservoir which feeds it.

Water soaks through some things (like sand and blotting-paper), but not through others (like clay and glass). Springs are formed where beds of clay slope down and reach the surface of the ground.

Some things (like salt and sugar) dissolve in water. Other things (like sulphur and charcoal) do not dissolve in water. Impurities which do not dissolve may be removed by filtering.

**Solutions**

Two kinds of stuff (one of which dissolves and the other not) may be separated by shaking up the mixture with water. The water may be poured off and the soluble stuff obtained by boiling away the water.

In any quantity of water only a fixed amount of a solid will dissolve.

Usually (but not always) much more of a solid will dissolve in hot water than in cold.

## Crystals

Crystals are formed when a warm saturated solution is allowed to cool. Crystals have regular shapes.

The more slowly the solution cools the larger are the crystals. Crystals that are larger still may be formed by allowing a cold saturated solution to dry up slowly.

Some kinds of stuff take up water when they form crystals. This "water of crystallization" may be driven off by heating. The stuff is then no longer crystals.

Crystals are also formed when a liquid freezes.

## Heated water

When water is heated air dissolved in it is driven out. When it is further heated, bubbles of steam form at the bottom and rise to the top.

Steam is invisible. On reaching the cold air it changes to a cloud of water particles. These particles soon change to invisible vapour again.

When water is heated it expands, so that warm water is lighter than cold water. When a jar of water is heated below, the lighter warm water below is pushed up by the heavier cold water above.

## Evaporation

Water evaporates (or dries up) at all temperatures. There is greatest evaporation: i. when the air is warm; ii. when the air is dry; iii. when the air is moving; iv. when the water surface is as great as possible.

When water dries up it takes heat from things about it without becoming warmer itself.

There is always some moisture in the air. When the air is sufficiently cooled some of this moisture falls as rain. Some kinds of stuff absorb moisture from the air.

## Water pressure

Water presses in all directions. At any point the pressure is at right angles to the surface on which the water presses, and it is the same in every direction.

Water pressure increases with depth. At a depth of one foot, for example, the pressure is 62 ½ pounds on each square foot, that is, the weight of the cube of water pressing on the square foot.

## Floating things

When a solid is in water the water supports some of the weight (equal to the weight of water displaced by the solid). If the solid is lighter than its own volume of water, the water supports the whole weight and the solid floats.

Floating things float so that they displace their own weight of water. An iron ship floats because the weight of water it displaces is not less than the weight of the ship. Salt solution is heavier than water. Hence things float higher in salt solution than in water.

## The elastic skin of water

Water behaves as if it had an elastic skin. The surface of water will support small weights.

Other liquids also behave as if they had an elastic skin.

Water rises in narrow tubes. The narrower the tube the greater is the height to which the water rises.

Soap solution forms thin elastic films (soap bubbles). The film always contracts so that it takes up the least possible space.

## CHAPTER III

# LESSONS ON ELECTRIFIED THINGS AND ON MAGNETS

### 1. Things electrified by rubbing

*Note:* Choose a dry day for experiments on electricity. Keep all the apparatus warm and dry. At home dry the things at the fire. At school they may be dried on a hot water radiator or over a gas flame.

The best day to choose is a hot dry day in summer.

**Experiment 1.** i. Tear up some scraps of paper and put them on the table. Dry a sheet of brown paper, place it against the wall or on the table, and brush it hard with a clothes brush. Then hold the sheet over the scraps of paper and lower it slowly. The scraps of paper will be seen dancing up and down between the table and the electrified sheet of paper.

ii. Electrify the sheet of paper by drying it and brushing it again. Hold it over a heap of fluffy feathers.

iii. Cut some thin strips of tin foil (from chocolate or cigarette boxes). Place them on the table and hold an electrified sheet of paper over them.

iv. Electrify the sheet of paper by drying it and then drawing it quickly under the arm several times with the arm pressed to the side. Then hold it over the scraps of paper.

**Experiment 2.** This is electric paper-hanging.

Dry a sheet of paper, place it against the wall, and brush it hard with a clothes brush. You will find that the electrified sheet of paper clings to the wall.

Several sheets may be fixed up in this way before the first sheet loses its electricity and falls.

**Experiment 3.** Tear up some slips of paper, and warm and dry them.

Take one piece, hold it flat on the table, and rapidly brush it with the knuckles four or five times. Then let it touch the face and it will stay there.

**Experiment 4.** This is a hair-raising experiment.

Electrify a sheet of paper by brushing it. Hold it over a boy's hair. (Choose a boy with rather long hair.) Some of the hair will rise up on end and will follow the paper as it is moved from side to side.

**Experiment 5.** Warm and dry a fountain pen and a piece of flannel. Rub the pen hard with the flannel. Then hold the pen over scraps of paper or over feathers to show that it is electrified. You may notice that some of the scraps of paper fly up to the pen and at once fly down again. This is because they become electrified themselves by the pen. Others lie along the pen as if they were joined to it.

Electrify the pen also by rubbing it on the coat sleeve.

Instead of the pen a vulcanite or ebonite rod or comb may be used.

**Experiment 6.** Warm and dry a glass tumbler and a silk handkerchief. Rub the tumbler with the handkerchief and then hold it over scraps of paper to show that it is electrified.

**Experiment 7.** Make some cork dust by cutting up or filing three or four corks.

Put the cork dust on a sheet of paper between two books of equal height. Warm a sheet of glass and place it across the books. (Figure 36.)

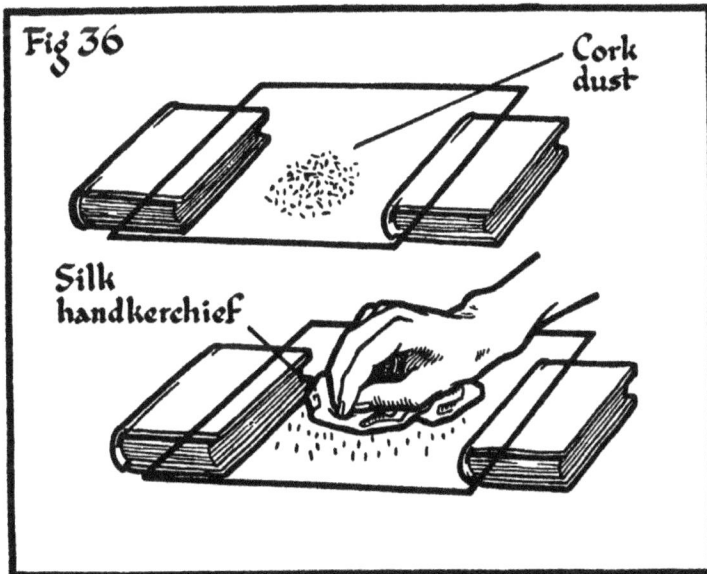

Rub the glass with a warm silk handkerchief. The cork dust will be drawn up to the electrified glass.

Thin strips of cork jump and dance and fly about most amusingly. To get the best results take the handkerchief away after rubbing.

## 2. *Things electrified in opposite ways*

**Experiment 1.** Cut out a piece of paper about this size and shape. Fold it back along the lines.

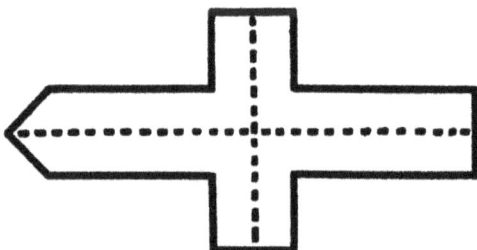

Push a pin up through a piece of cork. Place the pointer on the pin point. If it does not balance exactly cut off snips from the end which hangs down till it does balance. (Figure 37.)

Fig 37

Bring a glass tumbler rubbed with silk near the pointer. The pointer will swing round to it.

Bring up also a fountain pen rubbed with flannel, and a sheet of paper brushed with a clothes brush. Each attracts the pointer.

**Experiment 2.** Use the pointer described above.

i. Warm a fountain pen and rub it with warm dry flannel. Bring each in turn to the pointer.

It will be found that each draws the pointer, showing that each is electrified.

ii. Rub a glass tumbler with a warm silk handkerchief. Bring each in turn to the pointer. It will be found that the silk is electrified as well as the glass.

**Experiment 3.** Put the pointer on the table and over it put a warm dry tumbler. (Figure 38.)

Fig 38

Roll a silk handkerchief into a tight bundle. Rub the glass smartly at one point. The pointer will spin round to this point. In this way you may make the pointer point to any one near without raising the glass.

You may notice also that the pointer does not move to the electrified part of the glass till the handkerchief is removed. This is because the glass and the silk are electrified in opposite ways which balance each other.

**Experiment 4.** Tear two strips of paper each about two inches by six inches. Warm and dry them. Hold them with the fingers of one hand and rub them sharply between two fingers of the other hand. The electrified papers will fly apart. This is because they are both electrified in the same way. (Figure 39.)

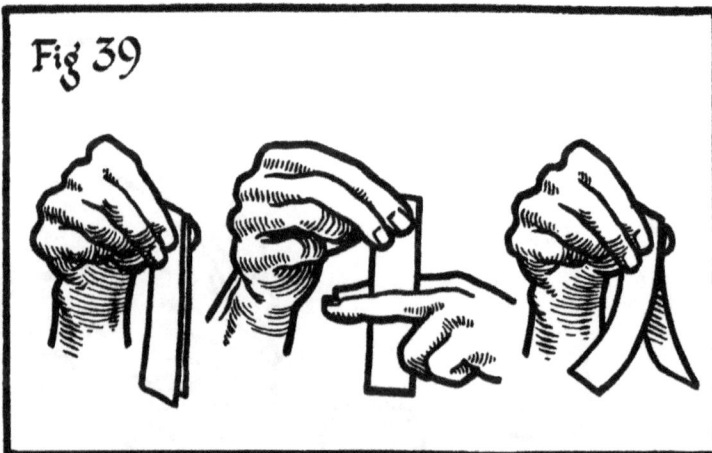

Fig 39

Hold the hand between the papers and they at once rush to it. Remove the hand and they fly apart again.

Repeat the experiment of holding an electrified vulcanite rod (e.g. a fountain pen rubbed on the coat) over scraps of paper. It will be seen that some of the papers fly away as soon as they touch the rod. This is because they are electrified in the same way as the rod.

**Experiment 5.** Tie a fluffy feather to the end of a piece of silk thread. Tie the other end of the silk to a support so that the feather hangs free.

Rub a fountain pen with warm dry flannel. Bring it near the feather. The feather will cling to the electrified pen. Draw the pen away. The hairs of the feather will be seen to stand apart. They repel each other because they are all electrified in the same way.

Now bring the pen slowly up to the feather again. You will find that it drives the feather away because feather and pen are electrified in the same way.

**Experiment 6.** Instead of the pen use a sheet of brown paper. Electrify the paper by brushing it.

Let the paper touch the feather, then draw it away, and afterwards bring it up slowly beneath the feather. The feather may easily be driven above the point from which it is hung because it is electrified in the same way as the sheet of paper.

**Experiment 7.** Electrify a suspended feather by letting it touch an electrified fountain pen.

Rub a glass tumbler with a warm dry silk handkerchief. Bring the glass slowly up to the feather but do not let it touch. You will find that the feather is drawn down to the glass, showing that the glass is electrified oppositely to the pen and the feather.

Bring up also the silk handkerchief. The feather is driven away, showing that the silk is electrified in the same way as the pen and feather.

Notice that the glass and the silk are electrified in opposite ways.

The pen and the flannel rubber may also be tested with the feather. It will be found that the pen drives the electrified feather away and the flannel draws it.

### 3. More experiments with electrified things

**Experiment 1.** Copy the little man on thin paper and cut him out. (Tracing paper will do.) (Figure 40.)

Fig 40

Electrify a fountain pen by rubbing it with flannel.

Hold the pen over the little man's head and raise him so that he stands on his feet. Draw the pen slowly along and the little man will come staggering after it.

**Experiment 2.** Copy the dancing lady and cut out the shape. Make a pin hole where the hands meet and put a piece of thread through it. Fasten the thread across the space between two piles of books or two chairs. (Figure 41 a.)

Fig 41a

Electrify a fountain pen by rubbing it with flannel. Hold the pen near the feet of the dancer. By moving the pen about, the dancer may be made to spin round on the thread.

**Experiment 3.** Make the swing with a match stalk and two pieces of thin silk thread. The girl on the swing is best made of paper with a fluffy feather for hair. (Figure 41 b.)

Electrify a fountain pen and hold it near the swing. The swing will be drawn toward the pen. Take the pen away while the swing is swinging to the opposite side. Bring it up when the forward swing is completed, and so on.

Fig 41 b

Two electrified pens may be used, one at each side of the swing, to increase the length of the swing.

**Experiment 4.** Hang up two feathers side by side by silk threads.

Electrify a fountain pen by rubbing it with flannel, and a glass tumbler by rubbing it with a silk handkerchief.

Electrify the feathers by letting the pen touch them. Remove the pen and the feathers will fly apart because they are electrified in the same way.

Bring up the pen slowly. The feathers will be driven still further apart.

Bring up the glass and the feathers will be drawn down to it.

In this way the feathers may be alternately drawn together and driven apart.

**Experiment 5.** Warm and dry a sheet of brown paper. Put the paper on the table and brush it vigorously with a clothes brush.

Raise the sheet from the table. A crackling noise will be heard and on a very dry day a shower of tiny sparks may be seen passing between the sheet of paper and the table.

**Experiment 6.** Warm and dry three glass tumblers. Place them at the corners of a triangle. Over the tumblers place a metal tray, and on the tray a sheet of warm dry brown paper. (Figure 42.)

Fig 42

Metal tray

Brush the paper vigorously with a clothes brush. Touch the tray. Then raise the brown paper without touching the tray again. Bring a knuckle slowly up to the tray. There will be a small snapping noise, a spark will pass between the tray and the knuckle, and a slight prickling feeling will be felt.

Put the paper back, touch the tray, remove the paper, bring a knuckle up to the tray again. Several sparks may be made in this way before the electricity has leaked away.

When you touch the tray, the electrified paper drives its own kind of electricity out of the tray and through your body, leaving the tray electrified with the opposite kind. It is this electricity that causes the spark.

### 4. Magnets—1

*Note:* A horseshoe magnet may be used for the following experiments, but bar magnets are better.

**Experiment 1.** i. Use a magnet to test what it attracts. Test small pieces of iron, steel, brass, etc. It will be found that the magnet attracts only iron and steel.

ii. Test also a tin lid. This is attracted. The "tin" is really iron covered with tin.

iii. Touch the magnet with a piece of iron. Notice that the magnet is drawn by the iron just as the iron is drawn by the magnet.

iv. See from what distance a magnet will draw small objects. Pins, needles, small nails, and large nails may be tested. Note that the smaller the object the greater the distance the magnet will raise it.

**Experiment 2.** Mix some brass pins and steel or iron pins. Use the magnet to sort them out.

Spill some iron pins on the floor and use the magnet to collect them.

**Experiment 3.** Get a small celluloid duck. Make a small hole in the top and drop in iron tacks, but not sufficient to sink the duck. Float the duck on a bowl of water.

The duck will then swim round after a magnet concealed in the hand.

**Experiment 4.** Put three or four pins or needles on the table. Over them place a sheet of paper. Place the end of a magnet on the paper above the pins. Raise the magnet and paper together. It will be found that the pins are raised with the magnet. The magnet attracts through the paper.

Move the magnet slowly along and the pins will follow it on the other side of the paper.

**Experiment 5.** Spread out some iron filings or small iron tacks on a sheet of paper. Place a magnet on them and then raise the magnet. It will be found that the filings or tacks cling to the ends of the magnet but not to the middle.

The places where most filings cling are called the "poles."

**Experiment 6.** Place a small piece of iron (a small bolt, or a short length of an iron bar, or a short length of thick iron wire) so that it touches one of the poles of a magnet.

Raise the magnet and iron together and let the iron touch some iron filings or small iron tacks. It draws them just as a magnet does.

Remove the magnet. The iron no longer draws the filings.

**Experiment 7.** Hang up a magnet by a piece of thread. (Figure 43.)

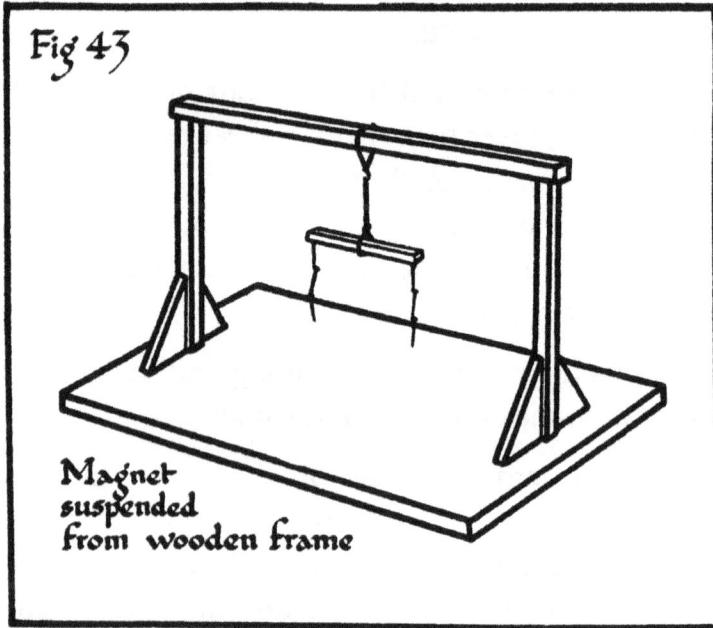

Fig 43

Magnet suspended from wooden frame

Place a pin so that it hangs down from one pole of the magnet. Place another pin so that it hangs from this, and then another pin below this. See how many pins you can hang up in this way. Notice that each of the pins behaves as if it were a magnet. You may also notice that they become weaker because you soon reach a point where no further pins will cling.

**Experiment 8.** Hang up a magnet so that it is level.

See how many pins or tacks you can get to cling one below the other at different points along the magnet.

You will find that the number is greatest at the poles, and less and less toward the middle.

If you use a horseshoe magnet you may find that the lowest pins swing together as if they were magnets.

## 5. Magnets—2

*Note:* Two bar magnets are needed for some of the following experiments, but knitting needles may be used.

Place a knitting needle flat on the table. Rub it from end to end with one pole of a magnet. Repeat five or six times, always rubbing with the same pole and in the same direction.

If the knitting needle loses its magnetism, it may be remagnetized in the same way.

**Experiment 1.** Use thread to hang up a bar magnet (or a magnetized knitting needle) at its middle point. Adjust the magnet so that it hangs level.

When the magnet comes to rest notice the direction in which it sets. (Pin a sheet of paper just below the magnet, and draw the direction of the magnet on the paper.)

Give the magnet a slight swing. You will see that it comes to rest in the same direction as before. Repeat this several times. It always comes to rest along the first line you drew.

Notice that the marked end of the magnet points

north. (Mark the north-seeking pole of the needle with a scratch or a scrap of gummed paper.)

**Experiment 2.** Magnetize a sewing needle by rubbing it from end to end with one pole of a magnet.

Place the needle carefully on the surface of water in a basin so that it floats. The floating needle will set north and south.

**Experiment 3.** Put a small compass flat on the table. Disturb it in various ways and notice that the needle always comes to rest in a north and south direction except when iron or magnets are near.

Place a piece of iron near the compass and notice that one end of the needle is drawn towards it. Also place a magnet near the compass and note how the needle is deflected.

**Experiment 4.** Use thread to hang up a bar magnet or a magnetized knitting needle.

i. Bring the poles of another magnet in turn slowly up to one pole of the suspended magnet. It will be seen that in one case the poles attract each other, and in the other case drive each other away.

Repeat this with the other pole of the suspended magnet.

ii. Bring a marked (north-seeking) pole slowly up to the marked pole of the suspended magnet. It will be seen that they drive each other apart.

iii. Show also that two south-seeking poles drive each other apart.

iv. Show also that a north-seeking pole attracts a south-seeking pole.

**Experiment 5.** Repeat the experiments with the poles of a magnet, using a small compass needle instead of the suspended magnet.

Try also the effect of trying to raise one magnet by means of another.

In each case you should find the same result: unlike poles attract each other; like poles repel each other.

**Experiment 6.** i. Magnetize a sewing needle by rubbing it from end to end with one pole of a magnet. Then float the needle on water.

The floating needle may be driven away, drawn along, turned round by presenting to it in turn the poles of a magnet. Do not bring the magnet too near.

ii. Instead of the sewing needle use a magnetized knitting needle. Float it by tying it to a thin strip of wood.

The knitting needle may be moved about in the same way as the sewing needle.

### *Summary: Science of electrified things and of magnets*

#### Things electrified by rubbing

Things electrified by rubbing attract small objects.

Vulcanite may be electrified by rubbing it with flannel, and glass by rubbing it with silk.

Both the rubber and the thing rubbed are electrified. They are electrified in opposite ways. The amounts of electricity produced are equal and opposite.

Things electrified in the same way drive each other apart. Things electrified in opposite ways attract each other.

Small sparks are produced when a finger is brought near an electrified tray.

## Magnets

Magnets attract and are attracted by iron and steel. They attract through paper and other things.

The greatest attraction is near the ends of the magnet—the "poles." There is little or no attraction at the middle.

If a magnet touches a piece of iron, the iron becomes a magnet so long as the magnet touches it.

A suspended magnet comes to rest in a north and south direction.

A piece of steel may be magnetized by stroking it with one pole of a magnet.

Unlike poles of magnets attract each other; like poles repel each other.

# CHAPTER IV

# LESSONS IN MECHANICS

## 1. How things fall

**Experiment 1.** Get several pieces of iron or lead or stone of different weights. Take in your hand two pieces of any of these, one piece being several times as heavy as the other. Stand on a chair and drop them together from as great a height as possible. Watch how they strike the ground. Do this several times—till you are sure that the two fall at the same rate.

Try other things in the same way. You should be quite sure before you stop that all the things you drop fall at the same rate.

**Experiment 2.** Hold a small tin lid and a feather side by side and drop them. You will see that the tin falls much more quickly than the feather. If you swing your arm round you may see that the reason is that the air checks the feather just as it checks your arm. It is easier to check the light feather than the heavy tin.

Now use the tin lid to clear the air out of the way for the feather. Put the feather on the lid, hold the lid level and drop it. You will find that the lid and the feather drop together.

Instead of a tin lid and feather use a penny and a piece of paper which nearly covers it.

**Experiment 3.** If you wish a thing to fall slowly give it a large surface for the air to press on. A parachute may be made from a large handkerchief. Tie strings to the corners, knot them together below to a piece of lead, iron, or other heavy stuff. Roll the parachute into a ball and throw it as high as you can in the air. At first it falls quickly, but as soon as it opens out the air checks it and it falls slowly. (Figure 44.)

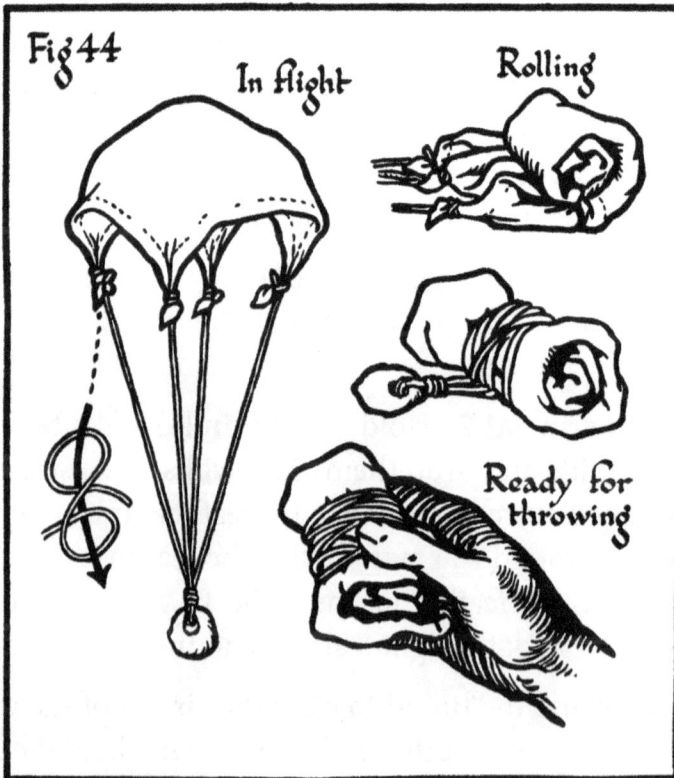

Fig 44 — In flight — Rolling — Ready for throwing

**Experiment 4.** Another kind of parachute may be made from two strips of thin paper, half an inch wide, and eight inches long. Place one strip over the other and twist them together about two-thirds of their length. Open out the tops and drop the little parachute from a height. It falls slowly, spinning as it falls. (Figure 45.)

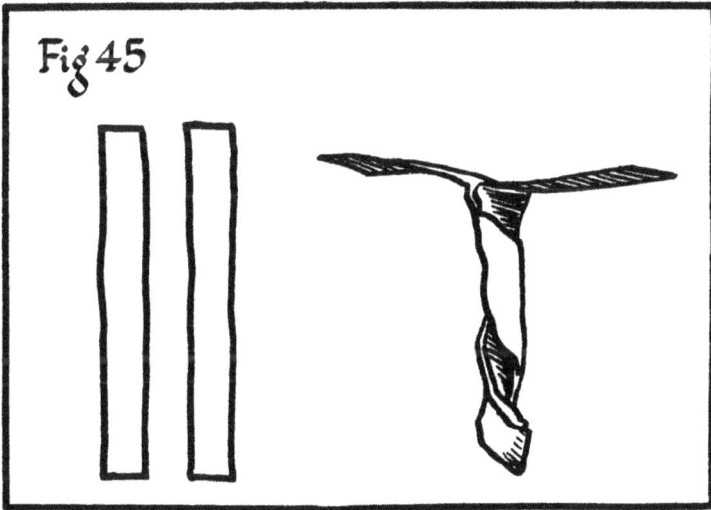

Fig 45

The reason for the spin is that the two sides are never exactly alike, and the air presses more on one than on the other. Try and make a card spin by giving it a sudden flick at one corner.

**Experiment 5.** Drop a small object into your hand from a height of a few inches, then from greater and greater heights. You will be able to feel that it falls quicker and quicker.

Try throwing up a ball and watching it come down. Throw it up a short distance, then greater and greater distances.

Try also throwing up a ball and letting it bounce. You will find that the greater the height from which it falls the greater is the bounce, and therefore the speed when it reaches the ground again.

**Experiment 6.** Throw up a ball as high as you can and watch how it rises more and more slowly, comes to a stop, and then falls more and more quickly. You might also try to draw the curve in which it moves.

A stream of water from a hose-pipe will also give the curve in which a falling body moves. Each drop of water moves in the curve that a solid body would take.

**Experiment 7.** Chalk a ball all over.

Hold a blackboard nearly upright and a ruler on edge close against it. Let the ball roll down the ruler. When it leaves the ruler it will trace out on the blackboard the curve along which it falls. (Figure 46.)

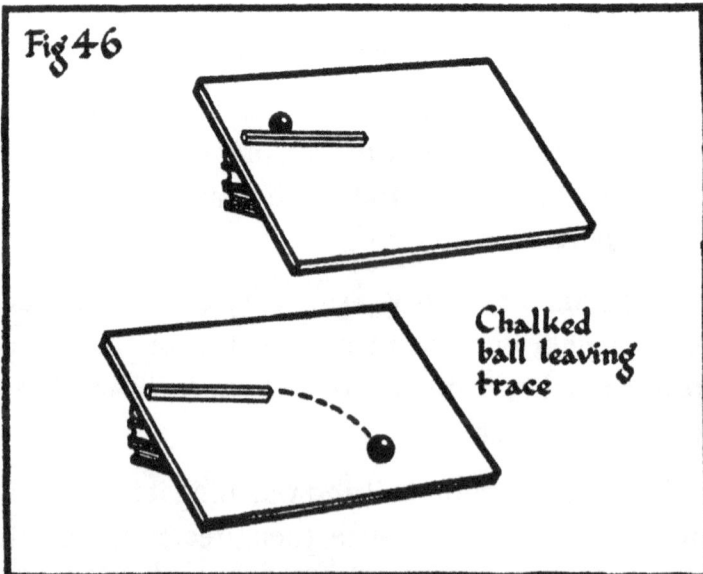

Fig 46

Chalked ball leaving trace

(Instead of a blackboard any board may be used, but the black shows up the white mark clearly.)

## 2. Pendulums

**Making pendulums.** A pendulum is made by tying a small weight to the end of a piece of string. Use thin string. The weights may be pieces of lead or small iron bolts.

Pendulums may be hung from steel eyes or from nails. If you are measuring the length of a pendulum measure from the point from which it is hung to the middle of the weight.

**Starting a pendulum.** When starting a pendulum swinging, hold it straight out and let go. Do not push it.

**Experiment 1.** Hang up two pendulums of equal length, one behind the other. Pull them out a little to one side and let them go at the same time. Now watch the pendulums from the front. You will see that they swing in the same time. Watch them for some time and notice that they continue to swing together.

Start the pendulums again, but this time hold one out farther than the other so that it has a longer swing. You will find that they still take the same time to swing. The length of the swing makes no difference to the time of swing.

Repeat this experiment with swings of different lengths, though none of them should be very great.

**Experiment 2.** Hang up three pendulums—a short one in front, a longer one behind it, and a still longer one behind that.

Start the front two pendulums together. You will see that the shorter pendulum swings more quickly than the longer one. Now start the longest pendulum swinging also. You will find that it takes longer still to swing.

**Experiment 3.** Hang up a long pendulum and set it swinging. Take the string between two fingers at the point where it is hung up. Run the fingers down the string. You will find that as the pendulum is shortened it swings quicker and quicker.

**Experiment 4.** Hang up three pendulums one behind another—the front one a foot long, the second four feet long, and the third nine feet long.

Start the front two pendulums together and count the swings. It will be found that the pendulum four times as long as the other, takes twice as long to swing.

Start the first pendulum and the third, and count the swings. It will be found that the pendulum nine times as long as the other, takes three times as long to swing.

**Experiment 5.** Hang up three other pendulums whose lengths are in the proportions 1 : 4 : 9 (e.g. 8 in., 32 in., 6 ft.).

It will be found that the times are in the same proportion as before—the second takes twice as long and the third three times as long as the first.

**Experiment 6.** Hang up two pendulums, one being sixteen times as long as the other (e.g. 8 in. and 128 in.).

It will be found that the second takes four times as long to swing as the first.

**Experiment 7.** Regulate a clock by changing the length of the pendulum. Find the effect of giving four upward turns to the nut below the pendulum. Then find the effect of giving it four downward turns.

Then change the length of the pendulum so that the clock shows correct time.

### 3. Levers

**Experiment 1.** Push a door open. It is quite easy when you push near the handle. Push half-way across the door, then three-quarters of the way toward the hinges, then seven-eighths, and so on.

You will find that as you get nearer to the hinges it becomes more difficult to move the door. You may also notice that to close the door, say, one foot, your hand moves one foot when it is at the outside edge, six inches when it is half-way across, and still less as you approach the hinges.

**Experiment 2.** Test in the same way lifting the lid of a desk, first at the outside edge, and then nearer and nearer to the hinges.

When you have the chance try raising one end of a heavy pole from the ground, first lifting at one end and then nearer the middle of the pole. If it is difficult near the end you may find that it is impossible near the middle.

**Experiment 3.** Drive a nail into a piece of wood. Then try to draw it out by means of a hammer. Pull on the hammer first close to the head, then half-way along the shaft, then at the end of the shaft. In the first position it is impossible to move the hammer, in the second it may be possible, in the third it is easier.

You may have noticed that in every case the easiest way to move a weight was by pressing at the end of a rod of some kind. The further from the turning-point you press, the easier it is to move the weight.

In the hammer note carefully where the turning-point is (where the hammer touches the wood). Notice also that in moving the nail, say, half an inch, the hand would move through twice the distance when at the end of the shaft that it would when at the middle.

**Experiment 4.** Use a pair of pincers to draw a nail. You will see that they are used in the same way as the hammer.

**Experiment 5.** Get a rod (any straight piece of wood) about two feet long. Tie string round the middle of the rod and hang it up. Adjust it so that it balances. (Figure 47.)

Hang a weight (say, one pound) at one end of the rod. Use a spring balance to find the force needed to raise this weight by pulling at various parts of the other arm. Put the ring or hook of the balance over the rod, support the weight, and note the reading on the balance.

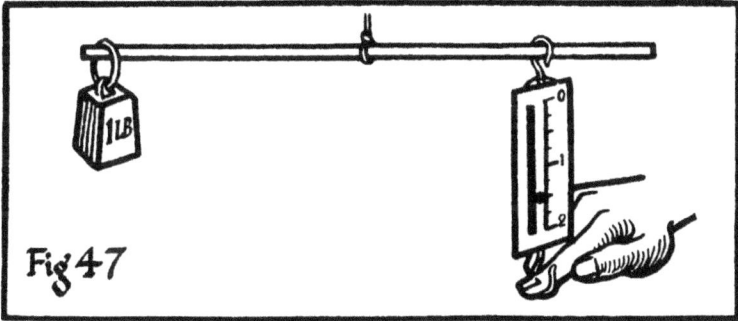

Fig 47

At the end one pound is required, half-way from the middle two pounds, one-third of the way from the middle three pounds, and so on.

You may notice that in every case:

Weight on one side **X** its distance from the turning-point = weight on the other side **X** its distance from the turning-point.

It is helpful to remember this. It will tell you the amount of force you have to exert in raising a weight by means of a lever.

**Experiment 6.** Get the strongest bar you can. (A window rod will do, but be careful in using it.)

Use the rod as a lever to raise a heavy weight (e. g. a heavy desk or cupboard). Put one end of the lever under the heavy weight, put a wooden block or brick under the lever close up to the weight, and press on the other end.

If the lever is very long, the pressure may break it. This is one of the limitations to the use of levers. Levers of this kind are usually stout iron bars, pointed so that they may be pushed under the object to be raised.

**Experiment 7.** Use any of the following as levers:

i. A tin-opener to open a tin.

ii. A screw-driver to remove a screw.

iii. A screw-driver to raise the lid of a tin.

iv. A brace and bit to bore a hole.

v. Nut-crackers to crack a nut.

In each case notice where the turning-point is, where pressure is applied, and where the weight is which is moved.

## 4. Balancing things—1

**Experiment 1.** i. Place a long rod on the finger. Move the rod about till it just balances on the finger. If the rod is even you will find that the balancing point is near the middle.

ii. You can get the point more exactly by balancing the rod on a knife edge. Mark this point.

iii. Put the rod on a table and slowly push it over the edge. As soon as the balancing-point moves over the edge, the rod tilts up and falls.

Notice that the rod behaves as if its weight were pulling at the balancing-point. This point is therefore called the centre of weight or gravity.

**Experiment 2.** i. Put a sheet of cardboard near the edge of a table. Push it slowly over the edge. Just as it is about to fall, hold it and draw along the edge of the table on the card. Notice that the centre of gravity is somewhere on this line because its weight would pull the card down when this line reaches the edge. (Figure 48.)

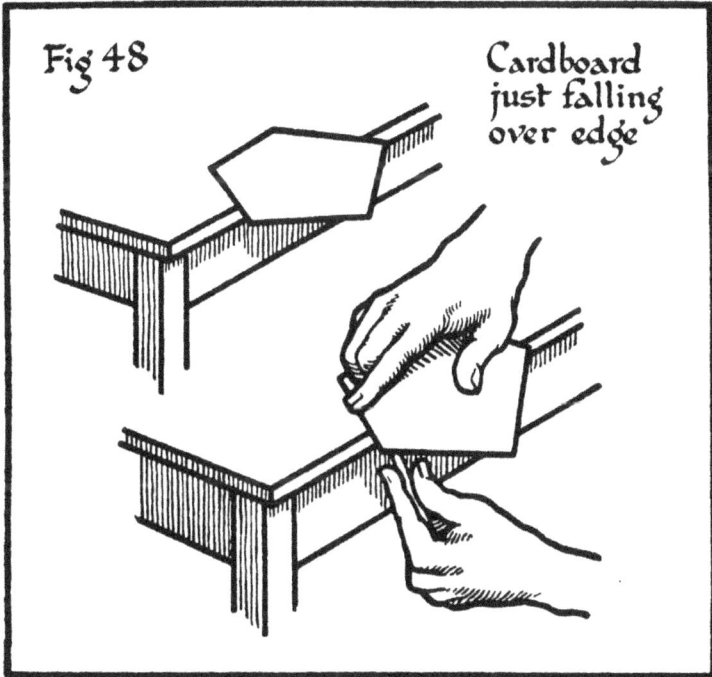

Fig 48

Cardboard just falling over edge

Turn the cardboard into other positions, and repeat the experiment. The lines should cross very nearly at the same point—the centre of gravity.

ii. The card may be balanced on a finger placed below it at the centre of gravity.

iii. Push a pin through the card at the centre of gravity. You will find that the card balances in any position about the pin.

**Experiment 3.** i. Cut out a circle in cardboard. Push a pin through it at the centre. The circle will be found to balance about the pin.

ii. Cut out a square and an oblong in cardboard. Show by balancing on a pin that the centre of gravity of each is where the diagonals cross.

iii. Cut out a triangle in cardboard. Draw lines from the corners to the mid-points of the opposite sides. Show by balancing on a pin that the centre of gravity is where these lines cross.

**Experiment 4.** Mark the centre of gravity of a sheet of cardboard, the cover of an old book, a thin piece of wood, and other flat objects. (Find the centres of gravity either by pushing them off a table, or by balancing them on the end of a knitting needle.) Make a hole near the corner of each object. (Figure 49.)

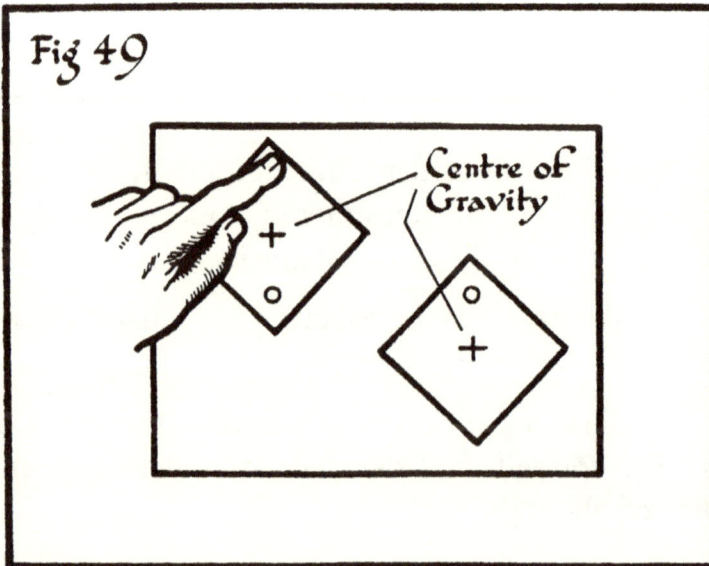

Fig 49

Centre of Gravity

Place one of the objects on a nearly upright board and fix it there by putting a nail into the board through a hole in the corner of the object.

Notice that the centre of gravity is exactly beneath the point at which the object is hung up. Move the object about. However you move it you should be able to see that the centre of gravity rises. When the object is at rest the centre of gravity is as low as possible.

Raise the object still touching the board. When you let go, it at once slides back to its old position as low as possible.

Test several objects in this way.

**Experiment 5.** Use the same objects as in the last experiment.

Raise one object till the centre of gravity is exactly over the point where it is fixed. With a little care you can balance it in this position. Give the object a slight push and it at once slides down till the centre of gravity is as low as possible.

Test various objects in various positions till you are sure that they will only balance in two positions:

i. With the centre of gravity as high as possible. This position is unstable because the object falls over if it is slightly disturbed.

ii. With the centre of gravity as low as possible. This position is stable. If the object is disturbed it at once moves back to its old position.

**Experiment 6.** Try to balance things with the centre of gravity high up. A poker or a walking-stick may be balanced on the finger, but they very easily lose their balance and fall.

**Experiment 7.** Try to balance a pencil on the finger. You will find it very nearly impossible.

Now lower the centre of gravity below the point of support. To do this open one blade of a penknife at right angles to the knife. Put the point of the blade into the pencil near the point. The pencil will now readily balance on the finger. (Figure 50.)

Fig 50

### 5. Balancing things—2

**Experiment 1.** Find the centre of gravity of a walking-stick, a flat board, a sheet of cardboard, by balancing them on a knife edge or the point of a knitting needle. Mark each centre of gravity.

Put the objects on a table and push them one by one over the edge. Each begins to fall as soon as the centre of gravity is not supported.

**Experiment 2.** Stand against the wall with one arm, leg, and foot pressed tightly against it. Then try to raise the other foot from the ground and hold it in the air. After some attempts you will probably decide that it is impossible, because you begin to fall over as soon as the foot is off the ground. (Figure 51.)

Fig 51

This is because your centre of gravity is over the edge of the thing you are resting on (in this case, the space your foot covers).

Now try again, holding a heavy weight in the hand touching the wall. If the weight is heavy enough you will be able to do it because the weight moves the centre of gravity (of yourself and the weight) nearer the wall.

**Experiment 3.** Stand near the wall, bend forward till your hands touch the ground. Move them forward as far as you can without falling over. Try and rise from this position without moving your feet. You will find that you cannot do it. Your centre of gravity is once more outside the base on which you are standing. (Figure 52.)

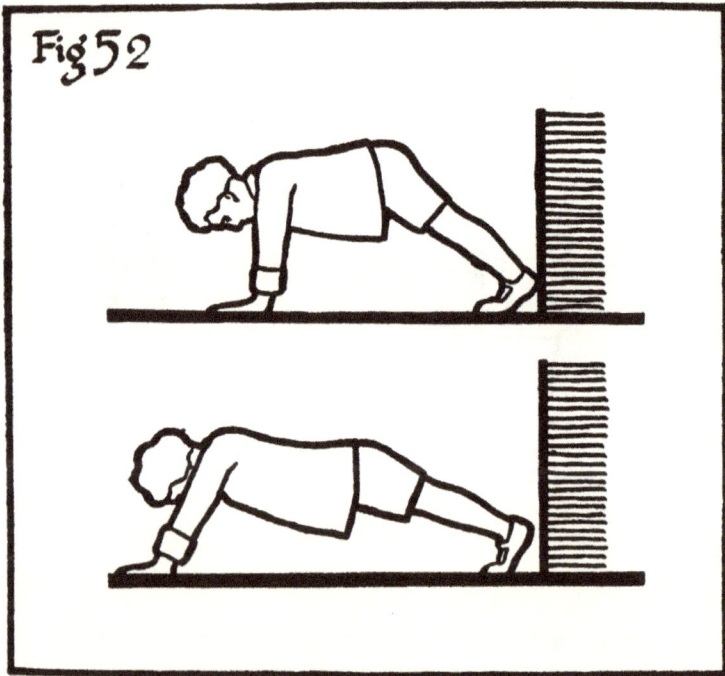

Fig 52

**Experiment 4.** If you have not a top-heavy vase use a tall narrow tin or anything tall on a very small base.

Tilt a top-heavy vase slightly, then more and more, till you find the point at which it begins to fall over.

Test a vase wide at the base (or a tin with a wide base) in the same way. You will find that the vase with a wide base requires to be tilted much more than the tall narrow one before the centre of gravity is outside the base and it begins to fall over.

Top-heavy vases are clumsy but they are easily knocked over and broken.

**Experiment 5.** i. Get a tall tin (like those used for lawn sand). See how far you can tilt it before it begins to fall.

ii. Load the tin with sand or bits of lead. You will find that you can tilt it much farther before it begins to fall over.

iii. Load the tin at the top by tying a piece of lead or iron there. You will find that you can hardly tilt it at all before it begins to fall over.

**Experiment 6.** i. If you have a toy cart see how far you can tilt it before it begins to fall over.

ii. Load the cart with heavy things (iron, lead, or stones). You will find that you can tilt it further.

iii. Load the cart again, piling the things up high. Boxes and wooden bricks may be used to load the cart. Tie them on with string. You will find that the cart will turn over more easily.

iv. Add weights to the top of the load and the cart will turn over more easily still.

When loading a cart the heaviest things should be placed at the bottom to lower the centre of gravity as much as possible. Look at a tramcar and you will see that the heavy machinery is placed low down to lower the centre of gravity as much as possible.

**Experiment 7.** Toys may be bought for a few pence at the toy shop which spring up no matter how they are placed. Lay one of these toys on its side. It at once springs up. Stand it upside down. It turns over and jumps up again.

Examine the toy. You will find that the base is made of lead. The top part is very light—celluloid or plaster. Even when the toy is lying on its side the centre of gravity is inside the base, and its weight pulls it upright.

If you have any difficulty in buying one of these toys you can make one. Pour melted lead into a small tin basin (the scale-pan of a pair of toy scales, for example). Then glue a small celluloid doll on top.

## 6. *When things rub together*

**Experiment 1.** i. Warm and dry a sheet of brown paper. Place it against the wall and rub it vigorously with a clothes brush. The sheet of paper sticks to the wall because it is electrified.

ii. Rub the sheet again and use it to raise scraps of paper.

One effect of rubbing things together is to electrify them.

**Experiment 2.** Rub the hands together. You will see that they become warm. This is another effect of rubbing.

**Experiment 3.** Get a piece of rather rough wood and a piece of sandpaper. Rub the fingers over each and notice the roughness of each.

Rub the wood vigorously with the sandpaper. You will see that both sandpaper and wood become warm.

After a time rub the fingers over the wood and the sandpaper again. You will feel that neither is so rough as it was at first. The little parts which stick out and make the roughness, rub each other away.

The wood may gradually be made very smooth. The sandpaper will lose its roughness so that it becomes useless.

**Experiment 4.** Get a piece of wood about eight inches long, and one or two inches square.

Leave one side rough and plane the other three. Mark the rough side "1".

Mark one of the planed sides "2". Rub the remaining sides with coarse sandpaper.

Mark one of the sandpapered sides "3". Rub the other with very fine sandpaper and mark it "4".

By feeling the sides with the fingers you will be able to see that there are four grades of roughness on them.

**Experiment 5.** Put a small hook in one end of the piece of wood prepared in the last experiment. Fasten a piece of string to the hook, and to the other end of the string fasten a scale-pan made from a tin lid. (Figure 53.)

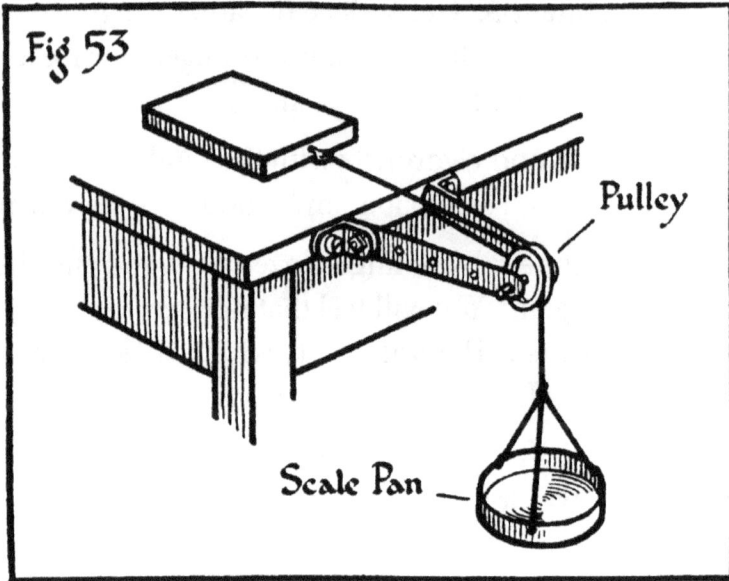

Fig 53

Pulley

Scale Pan

At the edge of the table fix a small pulley-wheel. (A convenient way of doing this is with Meccano parts.)

Place the wooden block on the table on its rough side. Pass the string over the pulley-wheel. Load the scale-pan with weights or small pieces of lead till the wood just begins to move.

Repeat with the wood on other faces. You will find that the smoother the face is, the less is the weight needed to draw the wood along.

**Experiment 6.** i. Try to slide on a rough pavement. The rough pavement stops your movement almost at once. It may stop your feet so suddenly, while the top part of your body goes on moving, that you fall over.

ii. On smooth concrete you will find that you can slide farther.

iii. On a slide made over ice or snow you will find that you can slide much farther still.

Notice that the rougher the surface the more it resists movement over it. There is nothing so smooth that it does not resist movement at all.

**Experiment 7.** Use the wooden block, pulley-wheel, and scale-pan suggested in Experiment 5.

Find the weight that will just move the wooden block when on its rough side.

Put another block of wood of the same size on top of the first block. You will find that it takes twice as much weight to move the block.

Put a third block over the others and you will find that it takes three times as great a weight to move it, and so on. (This is expressed shortly by saying that the force needed to pull a body over a surface on which it rests is proportional to the weight of the body.)

**Experiment 8.** Use the same block of wood again. Saw it in two, put the free half on the other, and find the weight needed to move it.

You will find that the weight is about the same, showing that the size of the surfaces rubbing makes no difference to the force needed to move the body.

## 7. *Inertia—1*

*a.* When things are at rest they do not begin to move unless they are pushed or pulled. Some amusing experiments may be tried to illustrate this.

**Experiment 1.** Place a card (a playing-card or a postcard cut in half) on the forefinger of the left hand. Over the card place a penny. Give a corner of the card a quick flick with a finger of the other hand. The card should fly out leaving the coin on the finger. (Figure 54.)

Fig 54

If the flick is not strong enough the coin will be moved too, because the card rubbing on the coin pushes it along with it. After a few trials you should be able to flick the card so strongly that it moves away without having time to move the coin more than a very small amount.

**Experiment 2.** Place a strip of paper over the edge of a tumbler. Over the paper balance a penny. Try to remove the paper and leave the coin.

If you pull gently the paper pulls the coin with it.

The best way is to hold the paper straight out and bring the hand down smartly on the middle of it. The sudden jerk will draw out the paper before the coin has time to move more than a very short distance.

**Experiment 3.** Try to remove a d'oyley from under some bread and butter on a plate, without moving the bread.

A quick jerk will remove the d'oyley before the bread has time to move far. The bread remains where it is because it has not been pulled more than a very short distance.

**Experiment 4.** Place a sheet of smooth paper on a smooth table. On the paper place some small objects. Choose rather flat objects which will not easily fall over—e. g. a plate, an empty ink-bottle.

A quick jerk will remove the paper and leave the objects on the table.

It is possible to remove a tablecloth in this way, but it requires some skill, and there is danger of a smash.

**Experiment 5.** Get a piece of tubing (glass or rubber tubing or a roll of paper). Fill the tubing with tobacco smoke and cover the ends with the fingers.

Hold the tube upright, open the ends, and lift the tube straight up. The smoke will be left behind as a column because it has not been pushed or pulled.

If the air in the room is still, the column of smoke will remain for a short time.

**Experiment 6.** Tie a piece of iron or lead to the end of a stick with thread.

Move the stick slowly and the weight is drawn along with it. Now give the stick a quick jerk. The thread will probably be broken before the weight has time to begin moving with the stick.

Apples are sometimes shaken down from trees in this way. A branch is bent forward and then suddenly jerked back. The joining is snapped before the apple has time to change its direction and begin moving with the branch.

When carpets are beaten, the carpet is pushed forward suddenly and the dust is left behind.

**Experiment 7.** Drive a nail through a light piece of wood. Turn the point of the nail up and put the wood across the space between two piles of books. Try to clinch the nail by driving it sideways with a hammer. You will find this difficult because the light wood and nail are easily moved by the hammer blows.

Now hold the head of another hammer below the nail and hammer again. The heavy hammer is only moved a little by the blows and so the nail can be flattened out against it.

A blacksmith uses a heavy anvil because this large mass is moved very little by the blows of his hammer.

## 8. Inertia—2

*b.* When an object is moving it will go on moving in a straight line unless it is pushed or pulled.

This is not so easy to see, but the idea can be illustrated by some easy experiments.

**Experiment 1.** Tie a small weight with a short piece of thread to the middle of a stick. Strike the end of the stick sharply on the ground. The ground stops the stick. The weight will probably go on moving with sufficient speed to break the thread.

If you are standing in a train or a tramcar, you will feel yourself thrown backward when it starts, because your body does not start to move at once. When the train stops, your body goes on moving and you are thrown forward.

**Experiment 2.** Strike a thin stick sharply on an iron railing or on the edge of a table. The stick will probably break, because the part near the hand is stopped whilst the other end goes on moving.

**Experiment 3.** Dip a small brush in water. Jerk the brush forward and stop it suddenly. The brush is stopped but the water goes on moving, and the ground will be spattered.

**Experiment 4.** Tie a small weight to the end of a piece of string. Hold the other end of the string in the hand and swing the weight round in a circle.

You will feel a pull outward on your hand. It is the pull of your hand on the weight that prevents the weight moving away. To show that this is so, let go the string. The weight at once flies off.

Try this experiment several times in a place where you are sure the weight can do no damage.

**Experiment 5.** Hold a wet umbrella open and spin it round quickly. You will see water flying off just as the stone flew off.

A wet mop may be dried by spinning it round in this way. Clothes are dried in laundries by putting them in a machine which spins rapidly.

Watch carriage wheels on a wet day. You will see mud flying off from them because there is not sufficient force to hold it to the wheels.

**Experiment 6.** Fill a small bucket nearly full of water. Hold it by the handle and swing it round in an upright circle. You will find that the water does not fall out of the bucket even when it is upside down. (Figure 55.)

Make a nail hole in the bottom of the bucket and you will see why the water does not fall out. Fill the bucket with water and swing it round again. As the bucket swings round water flies out of the hole.

When a tramcar or train is going round a curve passengers feel as if they are being flung outward. The

Fig 55

tramcar or train is pressed round by the rails, but the passengers go on moving in a straight line. Sometimes a tramcar jumps the rails and goes on in a straight line.

## Summary: Mechanics

### How things fall

Things fall at the same rate except when they are checked by the air. Air resistance only makes much difference when there is a big surface and a small weight.

As things fall they move quicker and quicker.

When a thing is thrown it moves in a curve called a parabola.

## Pendulums

The length of swing of a pendulum makes no difference to the time of swing.

The time of swing of a pendulum is proportional to the square root of the length of the pendulum, e.g. if one pendulum is 16 times as long as another, it takes 4 times as long to swing.

## Levers

The further from the turning-point of a lever you press, the less is the force required to raise a weight, but the greater is the distance you move to raise the weight a given distance.

The "moment" of a force about a given point is the product: force **X** distance from the point.

When a lever just balances, the moment of the weight at one side about the turning-point is equal to the moment of the weight at the other side about the turning-point.

## Balancing things

The point about which a thing balances is called its centre of gravity. When the centre of gravity is not supported the thing falls.

When a thing hangs freely from a point the centre of gravity is exactly below the point.

An object may be balanced with the centre of gravity exactly above the point of suspension, but this position is unstable. The balance is stable when the centre of gravity is exactly below the point of suspension.

Top-heavy things are easily upset because the centre of gravity is easily moved outside the base of the object.

## When things rub together

When things rub together each is electrified.

Each of the things also becomes warm.

When one thing rubs over another there is a force called friction which helps to check motion. This force is due to the roughness of the bodies.

The amount of friction does not depend on the size of the sliding surfaces. It does depend on the weight of the upper body. The weight required to move one body over another is a fixed fraction of the weight of the upper body.

## Inertia

Things do not move unless there is some force pushing or pulling them. If an object is moving it will go on moving in a straight line unless there is some force checking the movement or driving the object out of the straight line in which it is moving.

# CHAPTER V

# LESSONS ON LIGHT AND HEAT

### 1. A beam of light—1

These experiments should be tried in a room facing south and on a sunny day.

Cut a hole four inches square in a large sheet of brown paper. Pin the paper over the window. The room need not be quite dark, but make it as dark as you conveniently can.

**Experiment 1.** i. Notice that the outlines of the beam of light are only visible because of specks of dust in the air. Examine the beam carefully and you will see that it is full of dust. The beam is visible because the specks of dust throw some of the light back to the eye.

ii. Compare the appearance of the beam of light with the bright spot where more light is thrown back by the floor or wall.

iii. Hold a sheet of white paper in the beam of light. Notice that the spot of light on this is brighter still, because the white paper throws back more light than the wall or floor.

iv. Hold a piece of smouldering paper so that the smoke passes through the beam of light. It at once appears brighter, because there are more particles of dust to throw back the light.

v. Examine the edges of the beam of light when it is full of smoke. You should be able to see that they are quite straight.

**Experiment 2.** Cover the hole in the brown sheet with a piece of paper with a smaller hole in it (say, an inch across).

i. Light up the narrow beam with smoke and notice that it is straight.

ii. Let two pupils hold a piece of thread, one end at the opening where the light comes in, and the other end where the light falls on floor or ceiling.

Hold the thread straight out, keeping the fingers out of the beam of light. The thread will be seen lighted up along its whole length.

Let the thread slack a little and it at once disappears, because it is no longer in the straight beam.

**Experiment 3.** Place a mirror where the broad beam of light can fall on it. Notice how the beam of light is reflected from the surface of the mirror.

Smoke from smouldering paper will show that the two parts of the beam are each straight. You may also be able to see that the angle at which the beam hits the mirror is equal to the angle at which it is reflected.

**Experiment 4.** i. Place two pieces of looking-glass in the broad beam of light so that they reflect two spots of light on the ceiling. Notice that the spots are of equal brightness.

ii. Move one of the pieces of looking-glass till the spot of light reflected from it is some distance from the other. Then hold another piece of looking-glass in this reflected beam and reflect it again so that it is beside the first. You may be able to see that the light twice reflected is less bright than that once reflected.

iii. Let another pupil hold a piece of looking-glass so that one beam is three times reflected, then reflect it four and five times. You will see that the spot of light becomes dimmer after each reflection, showing that the mirror only reflects part of the light.

**Experiment 5.** i. Place a sheet of white paper in the beam of light. You will see that light is reflected from it, but the reflected light is more scattered than from the mirror. The spot of light on the wall or ceiling is much more vague.

ii. Place other sheets of paper in the beam of light. Try light brown, dark brown, and black paper, as well as various colours. You will see that the brighter the colour the more light is reflected from it. From the black paper hardly any light is reflected.

**Experiment 6.** Hold a mirror so as to throw a spot of light on the ceiling. Hold other mirrors so as to throw light on the same place. The spot becomes brighter and brighter as more and more light falls on it.

## 2. A beam of light—2

**Experiment 1.** Cover the hole through which light enters the room with a piece of brown paper in which is a hole an inch square.

i. Place a basin of water in the beam of light. When the water is still, look for the spot of reflected light on the ceiling. Touch the surface of the water to make it uneven. The reflected light is at once scattered.

Leave the water to become still again. The reflected light comes together again till there is once more a clear bright spot of light.

ii. Place a sheet of glass in the beam of light. You will find that light is reflected from this also without being scattered.

iii. Place a piece of glass and a mirror side by side in the larger beam of light. You will see that much more light is reflected from the mirror than from the glass.

**Experiment 2.** i. Fix a piece of red glass over the small hole (one inch square). Red light comes through the glass. This can be seen where the beam of light falls on the floor or wall.

Put a piece of red material in the red beam of light. The material looks red. Put other colours in the beam of light. Blue and green things look nearly black. This is because they do not reflect red light. Purple appears red because it reflects red light. White appears red because it reflects red light.

ii. Fix a piece of blue glass over the hole. In blue light blue material appears blue; red and yellow appear nearly black because they do not reflect blue light; purple appears blue because it reflects blue light as well as red; white appears blue because it also reflects blue light.

iii. Use glasses of other colours. It will be found that white material reflects all the colours.

**Experiment 3.** Place a basin of water where a narrow beam of light can fall on it. You will see that some of the light is reflected from the surface of the water.

Look into the water and you will see that part of the light passes through the water. You will also be able to see that the beam of light is bent down where it enters the water.

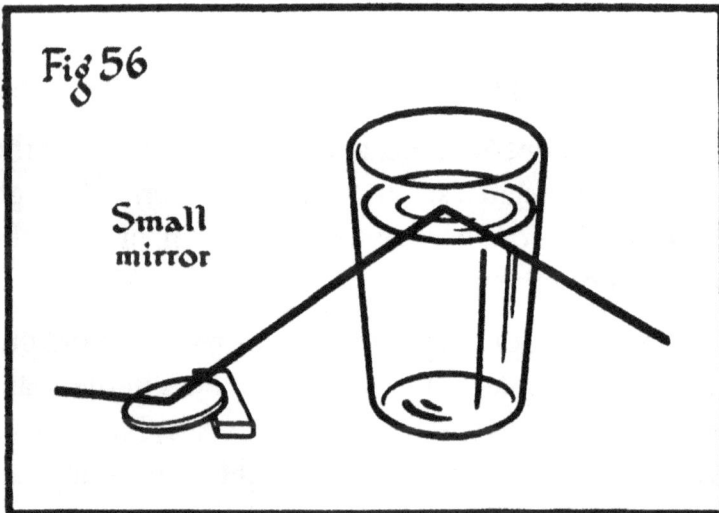

Fig 56

Small mirror

**Experiment 4.** Place a tumbler of water where you can reflect a beam of light upward through it. (Figure 56.)

Use a mirror to reflect a narrow beam of light upward through the water. Reflect the beam of light as nearly as you can from below. You should be able to see the beam of light passing through the water and bent down where it leaves the water.

Now throw a beam of light up through the water at a smaller angle with the surface. You will see that the whole of the light is reflected at the under surface and that none of it comes through.

**Experiment 5.** Cut a narrow slit in a postcard and fix this over the hole that admits light. (Figure 57.)

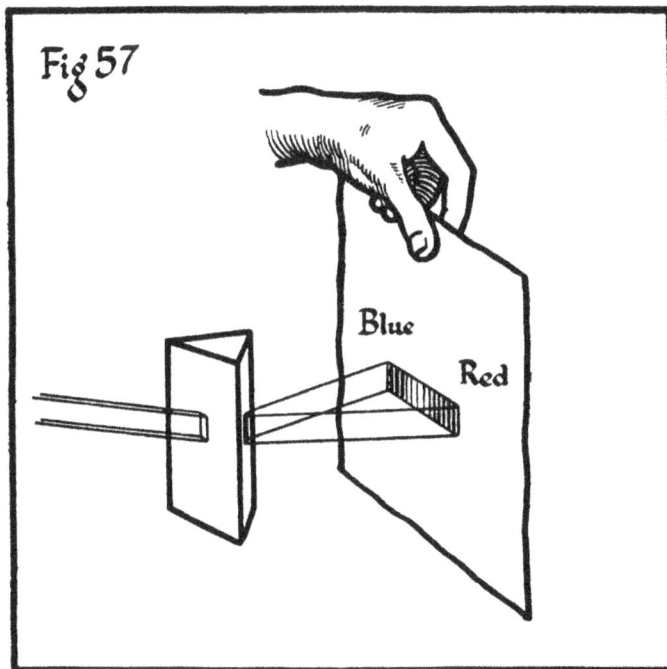

Fig 57

Blue

Red

Place a triangular glass prism upright so that the narrow beam of light falls on one face of it. Hold a sheet of white paper at the other side of the prism as a screen. The narrow white beam appears on the screen as a band of colours—red, orange, yellow, green, blue.

Examine the beam of light carefully. You will see that as it passes through the prism it is bent toward the base of the prism. You will also see that the blue is bent most and the red least.

### 3. Reflections

**Experiment 1.** Fix a small mirror upright.

i. Place a small object in front of it. You may be able to see that the reflection appears as far behind the mirror as the object is in front of it. Place four or five objects, some close to the mirror and others further away. The further away the object is from the mirror, the further back the image appears in the mirror.

ii. Place a small object close to the mirror. Then slowly draw it back. Notice how the reflection moves back into the mirror. Move the object to one side. The reflection moves with it.

**Experiment 2.** Use a set-square to draw two lines at right angles on a sheet of drawing-paper. Pin the paper on the table and place a mirror exactly along one line.

Look at the reflection of the line in the mirror. You will see that the line and its reflection appear as one line. (Figure 58.)

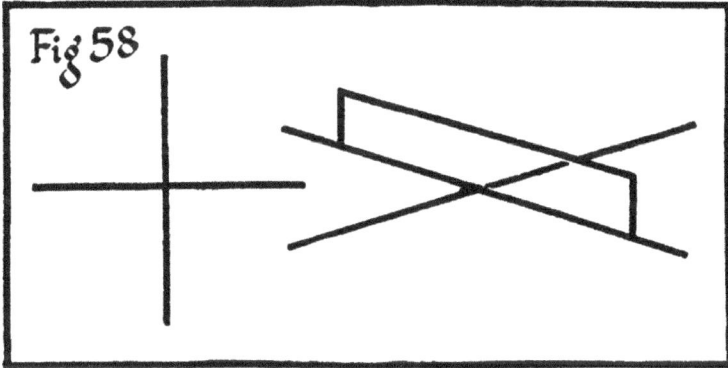

Fig 58

Place a small object at the end of the line. The line joining the object and its reflection crosses the line of the mirror at right angles.

**Experiment 3.** Fix a small mirror upright on a sheet of drawing-paper. Make two dots on the paper. Place the point of a pencil on one dot, and looking only at the reflections in the mirror try and join the dots.

The difficulty in doing this is owing to the fact that the line and its reflection slope in opposite directions.

Looking only in the mirror try and draw shapes which will be reflected as letters A, F, S, etc.

**Experiment 4.** i. Place two mirrors at right angles to each other. Put a small object in the angle between them. You will be able to see three reflections. The third reflection is not so bright as the others. It is caused by light which has been twice reflected, once from each mirror. A short length of burning candle will show the difference in brightness very clearly. (Figure 59.)

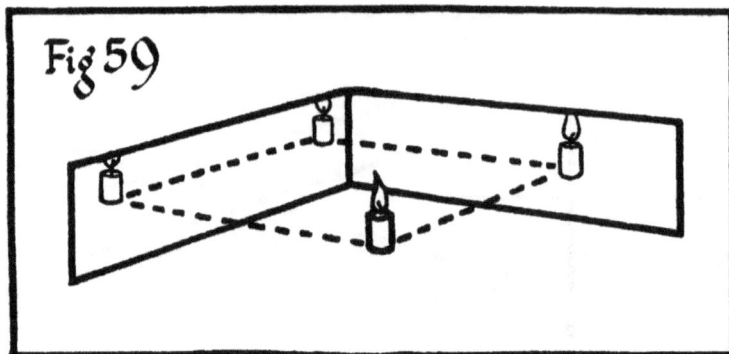

Fig 59

ii. Slowly move the mirrors so that the angle between them is less. A fourth reflection will appear, then a fifth, and so on. You will be able to see that the reflections are dimmer and dimmer as the light is reflected more and more often.

**Experiment 5.** Stand in front of a large mirror with a lighted candle in one hand and a hand-mirror in the other.

Turn the hand-mirror slowly and watch the reflections of the candle. The first is quite bright, the one behind it is less bright, the next is dimmer still, and so on.

With a little care you can hold the mirror so that a great number of reflections are seen, each less bright than the one in front of it. Light from the candle is thrown backward and forward between the mirrors giving a fresh reflection each time.

**Experiment 6.** Place a basin of water on the table, and near it a large vase or other tall object.

Look down into the water and you will see a faint reflection of the object. Now bring the eye slowly down to a level with the surface of the water. The reflection will become clearer and clearer till the eye is almost on a level with the surface of the water.

Very clear reflections may often be seen in sheets of still water. The reflections are clearest when you are a little way off so that the reflected light almost grazes the surface of the water.

**Experiment 7.** Fix a sheet of glass upright at the dark side of a room where little light comes through the glass from the back.

Look into the glass and you will see a reflection of yourself and things round about, but not very bright.

Move round to the side of the glass so that the reflected light comes up flatly from it and a much brighter reflection will be seen.

## 4. The refraction of light

**Experiment 1.** Place a basin on a table. Put a coin in the basin. Stand back from the basin so that you can just see the coin. Then stand further back so that it is just out of sight. (Figure 60.)

Fig 60

Get some one to pour water into the basin, taking care that the coin is not moved. You will see that the coin gradually comes into sight. This is because the rays of light from the coin are bent down where they reach the surface, so that they reach the eye.

**Experiment 2.** Fill a basin with water and place it on the table. Hold a stick slanting in the water. It will be seen that the stick appears bent. The part under water appears to be bent up. Again this is because rays of light are bent down where they reach the surface of the water. (The part of the stick under water is seen along the line on which the rays reach the eye.)

Hold the stick upright and it will be seen that the part under water appears shortened but not bent. This explains why water is really deeper than it appears.

**Experiment 3.** Place a sheet of thick glass on paper ruled with parallel lines. Look through the glass from one side. It will be seen that the part of the line under the glass does not appear in line with the rest of the line. It appears a little further away. This is owing to the bending down of the rays of light where they leave the glass.

The thicker the glass the greater will the distance between the parts of the line appear. This may be shown very clearly by placing a plano-convex lens on the lines. The part under the glass will appear to be bent out in a curve (that is, it is bent more and more as the glass becomes thicker).

**Experiment 4.** Get a glass tumbler with a thin base. Fill it with water and place it on lined paper. It will be seen that the paper under the water appears raised and that the lines appear further apart.

Cut a circle out of the paper so that the remainder of the paper can be raised round the tumbler. Raise the paper slowly until the parts of the lines outside appear in line with those inside. This will show the amount the bottom of the tumbler appears raised.

**Experiment 5.** Place a triangular glass prism upright on the table. Fix two pins upright in the table in a line making nearly a right angle with one side. Bring your eye down to a level with the pins (close one eye), and move about till you see one pin behind the other. Then fix two more pins in the table on the same side of the prism as the eye so that all four pins appear in a line. (Figure 61.)

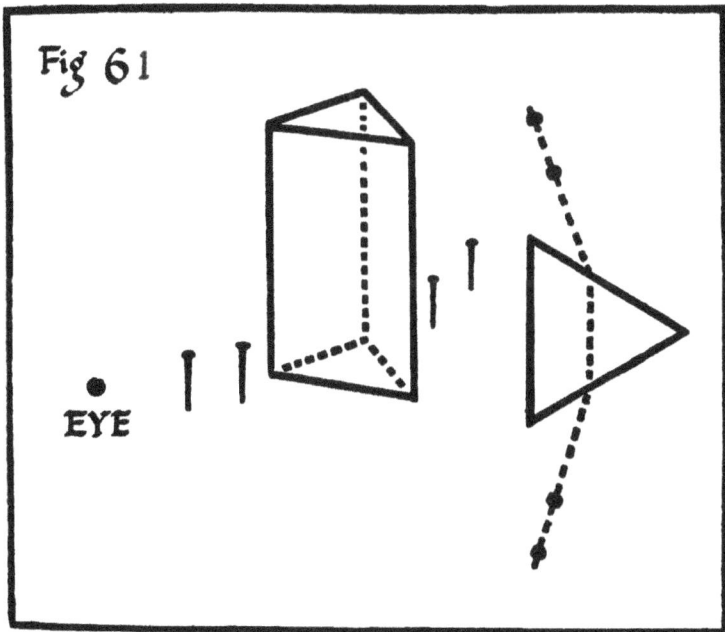

Fig 61

EYE

Draw round the prism and remove it. Join the first two pins by a straight line and continue it to the prism. Draw through the other pins in the same way. Then join the ends of the lines through the prism. The lines show the course of a ray of light through the first two pins, through the prism, through the other pins to the eye.

It will be seen that the ray of light is bent twice toward the base of the triangle, once when it enters the glass and again when it leaves the glass.

**Experiment 6.** Fill a tumbler with water and place in it a small rod. Hold the tumbler above the level of the eye. Look up through the water from below. The rod will be seen passing out through the surface of the water. (Figure 62.)

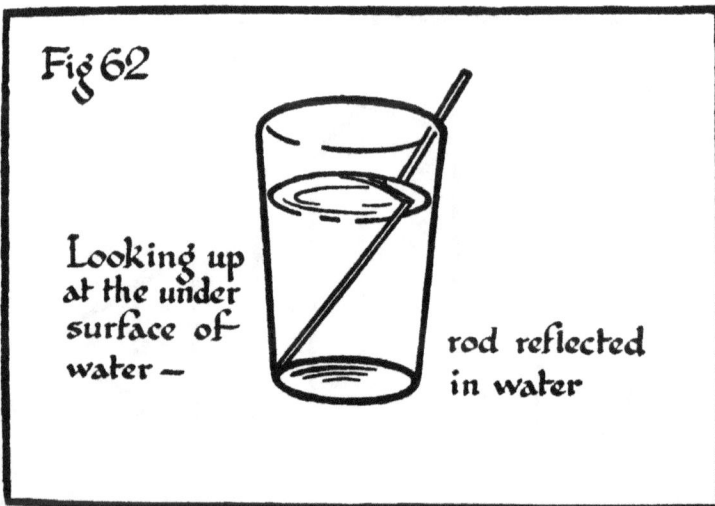

Fig 62

Looking up at the under surface of water —

rod reflected in water

Now hold the tumbler a little away and look up at the under surface of the water from one side. You will find that you can no longer see through the surface of the water. Instead you will see a clear reflection of the part of the rod which is beneath the surface of the water.

## 5. *How heat travels*

**Experiment 1.** Put a poker in the fire (or fix up the poker so that one end of it can be heated in a gas-flame).

Heat one end of the poker and touch the other end with the fingers occasionally. It will be felt that the end away from the flame soon begins to be warm. The heat can only come along the rod, because other things near the rod are not nearly so warm.

Run a finger carefully along the rod. Notice that the rod becomes hotter as you go nearer to the flame.

**Experiment 2.** A metal rod (especially a copper rod) can be used to carry heat from a flame to heat water at a little distance. (Figure 63.)

Fig 63

Fix up a rod so that it slants down into a jar of water and so that the upper end may be heated. Shield the water from the flame by means of a sheet of cardboard through which the rod passes.

Take the temperature of the water. (If no thermo-meter is available test the hotness by putting a finger in the water.)

Heat the upper end of the rod, and from time to time take the temperature of the water. It will be found that the water gradually becomes warmer as heat is carried down to it by the rod.

**Experiment 3.** Fill a jar with boiling water. In it place a metal spoon and a wooden spoon (or a wooden rod). After a little time feel the ends of the spoons. Heat quickly passes along the metal spoon and the whole of it becomes hot. The end of the wooden spoon remains cool.

**Experiment 4.** An amusing way of showing the difference between wood and copper as conductors of heat is to stick paper round a copper rod and round a wooden rod. Hold each in a gas flame. The paper round the wooden rod is scorched at once, whereas the paper round the copper rod remains unscorched.

In the case of the copper rod, heat is so quickly carried away by the copper that the paper remains cool, and the layer of gas just touching it does not become hot enough to burn.

**Experiment 5.** Heat travels badly through water. This is difficult to show because if water is heated below the heated water is pushed up by the heavier cold water round. The heated water itself moves. If water is heated above, however, the hot water remains where it is.

Fill a jar with cold water. Weight a piece of ice (one way is by tying it up in muslin with a piece of lead—but so that it can be seen), and sink it in the water.

Pour some spirits into a tin lid, float it on the water, and set fire to the spirits (or pour boiling water into a deep tin lid floating on the water). It will be found that though the water at the top is quite hot the ice does not melt.

This experiment may be done with a test-tube. (Figure 64.)

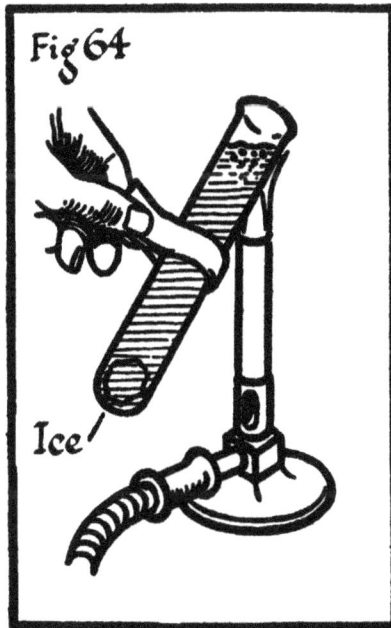

Near the equator the surface waters of the sea are heated by the sun. This heat does not travel down very far, and the water at the bottom of the ocean is ice cold.

**Experiment 6.** Heat also travels badly through gases. This is still more difficult to show because gases move readily when heated. But try the following experiments:

i. Fluffy materials contain a lot of air. They are bad conductors.

Wrap a piece of ice loosely in flannel. Leave a similar piece of ice exposed. When the exposed ice has melted examine the other piece. You will find it still unmelted because heat does not quickly pass through the flannel.

ii. Fill two similar tin cans with hot water. Wrap one tin in flannel and leave the other exposed. After fifteen minutes test the heat of the two lots of water by putting a finger in each. It will be found that the water in the covered tin is hotter. Less heat has been able to pass out of it because of the flannel.

**Experiment 7.** Fold over the edges of a paper-bag. Put three strings equally spaced through the folded paper and tie them together above.

Fill the bag with water and hold it over the gas flame. Take care that the flame does not touch any part of the paper above the level of the water.

It will be found that the water boils without the paper scorching. The water keeps a thin layer of gas cool enough not to burn. This layer of gas prevents heat reaching the paper quickly enough to scorch it.

**Experiment 8.** Hold the hands near a fire or near a gas-burner. The heat of the fire is felt very quickly.

Get some one to hold a newspaper between your hands and the fire. The heat of the fire is cut off at once.

Notice also that you can feel the heat of the fire even when the air is cool and fresh. Heat reaches the hands from the fire without heating the air between.

There is a great difference between the two ways in which heat travels. In conduction one heated part heats the parts touching it, these heat the parts touching them, and so on. In radiation heat is sent out in all directions without warming what it passes through.

Heat from the sun passes through space. It then passes through the air without warming it (the upper air is very cold), and finally warms the earth.

**Experiment 9.** Let a lump of lead lie on the ground in full sunshine for half an hour. When you pick up the lead it may be too hot to hold. This is so even when the air is rather sharp. (Any dull metal will do instead of lead.)

Notice in this case also that the sun's heat travels through the air without warming it.

**Experiment 10.** Fill a jar with water and drop a little sawdust into it. Put a small flame under the jar. The sawdust will show the movements of the water. The heated water near the middle is pushed up by the heavier cold water which presses in from the sides.

The heated water carries heat from the flame to the surface so that the whole of the water is evenly heated.

Compare this experiment with Experiment 5.

**Experiment 11.** Light a small gas flame and hold a piece of smouldering paper near it. The smoke will show the direction of air currents. The heated air above the flame is pushed up by cold currents pushing in from the sides.

Currents of heated air or water produced in this way are called convection currents.

## 6. *Ways of getting a light*

"How came she by that light?"—*Macbeth*

**Heat by rubbing.** Fire is one of the most important things in our lives. It would be interesting to work out the different ways in which fire affects our lives—light, warmth, cooking, manufactured things.

One way of obtaining heat is by rubbing.

**Experiment 1.** Rub the hands briskly one over the other. Notice that they become warm.

**Experiment 2.** Rub a brass button briskly on the sleeve. Touch the cheek with it. The button may be made hot enough to burn the skin. A better effect is obtained by holding the button with a piece of flannel or fixing it in a cork holder. (Heat does not pass quickly through flannel or cork.)

**Experiment 3.** Some peoples obtain fire by rubbing two sticks together. Rub two dry sticks together and you will find that you can make them quite hot. The following is a better method. It is quite easy by this method to char the wood, and with a little skill and patience you may obtain sparks. (Figure 65.)

Fig 65

Sharpen one end of a straight piece of stick. Tie a piece of string round it at the middle point. Wrap the string round the stick so that it can be pulled out at either end. Put the sharpened end of the stick in a slight hollow in a piece of wood on the floor. Use the body to press the stick down tightly. (The upper end may be held in another piece of wood or a small tin.) By pulling the string first at one side and then at the other the stick may be spun round rapidly. Smoke will rise from the point and the wood will be charred.

**Experiment 4.** Strike a match. Notice that in this case only slight heat is needed to fire the stuff on the head of the match. This heat is obtained by rubbing the match.

Use matches which strike anywhere. Strike them on various things. Notice that a longer sweep is needed on a smooth thing like glass than on a rough thing like sand-paper. A match is easily struck on a sheet of writing-paper because it sinks in slightly and makes a rough path for itself.

**Experiment 5.** Where two things rub together they become hot. To reduce the heating the things are made smooth by pouring on oil. Wheels, for example, are oiled where they turn on an axle.

Rub a knife on an oilstone as if you were sharpening it. Touch the knife and notice how hot it becomes. Now pour oil on the stone and rub the knife again. It does not become nearly so hot.

When a cart goes down hill with the brake on, notice how sparks fly from the part where the wheel rubs on the ground.

**Heat by striking. Experiment 6.** Knock one piece of flint against another, striking it a glancing blow. You will find that you can obtain sparks in this way. These are tiny pieces of flint broken off and heated white-hot by the blow.

**Experiment 7.** A better effect is obtained by striking flint with a piece of steel. With a little skill you can send the sparks where you wish. Prepare a piece of tinder by charring linen over the gas or fire. Direct the sparks on this and you may make it smoulder. By blowing the smouldering tinder a flame may be obtained which will set fire to a piece of paper.

Examine and use a flint and steel pipe-lighter. It is easy to obtain a shower of sparks from this and to coax the glowing tinder into a flame. The sparks are white-hot particles of steel.

Hammer a nail vigorously into a piece of wood and then touch the head of the nail and the hammer. You will find that they are both hot.

A better effect is obtained by hammering a punch into stone. The end of the punch becomes very hot.

**Heat by compression. Experiment 8.** Use a large garden syringe for this experiment. It should be in good working order and the leather collar well soaked so that there is little leakage. Raise the plunger and then carefully close the outlet by pressing it into plasticine on the floor. Drive the plunger down hard. You will find considerable resistance. Put your hand on the lower part of the barrel of the syringe and notice that it has become warm. This is due to the compression of the air in the barrel.

It may be better to have some assistance in doing this experiment. One boy or girl can hold the syringe and feel how it becomes warm whilst the other drives down the plunger.

If a hand is held tightly over the opening, steaminess will be noticed after the compression. The air cools again when it expands.

**Collecting heat with a lens. Experiment 9.** Try this experiment on a hot sunny day.

Scorch a piece of linen or cotton rag and then take it into the sunlight. Hold a lens over the rag. It will be seen that the light is collected to a small bright spot or focus. Move the lens till this spot is as small as possible. Then hold the lens steady. Smoke will be seen to rise from the rag. After a time it may begin to burn and it may be coaxed into a flame by blowing.

## *Summary: Light and Heat*

**Light**

A beam of light is only visible when it reaches the eye either directly or after reflection.

Rays of light are straight.

When a beam of light is reflected from a mirror both parts of the beam are straight. The angle at which light is reflected is equal to the angle at which it reaches the mirror.

Light may be reflected many times. Each reflection is less bright than the preceding one.

Paper scatters the light which falls on it. White paper reflects more light than dark paper. Black things reflect hardly any light.

Water and plain glass reflect less light than a mirror.

Through red glass only red light passes, through blue glass only blue light, etc. Red material reflects only red light, blue material only blue light, etc. White material reflects all colours.

When light passes into water it is bent toward the perpendicular to the surface. This bending is called refraction. Light which strikes the water surface at a small angle from below is totally reflected.

In passing through a triangular prism white light is broken up by refraction into the colours—red, orange, yellow, green, blue.

The reflection of an object in a mirror is the same distance behind the mirror that the object is in front of it. Two mirrors at right angles give three reflections, the third reflection being due to light twice reflected—once at each mirror.

Only part of the light which falls on a mirror is reflected. The smaller the angle at which light strikes the mirror the greater is the amount of light reflected.

**Heat**

Heat travels along rods. As each part is heated, it heats the parts close to it. This method of travelling is called conduction.

Metals are good conductors of heat. Wood, paper, flannel are bad conductors.

Water is a bad conductor. This fact is usually hidden by the fact that heat is carried up from below by convection currents.

Air and other gases are bad conductors. This is shown by the fact that fluffy materials (containing much air) are bad conductors.

Heat also travels (by radiation) without heating the material (air) through which it travels.

Things may be heated and fire obtained by rubbing things together.

Other methods of obtaining fire are by striking and by collecting heat rays from the sun with a lens.

When air is compressed it is heated.

## CHAPTER VI

# LESSONS ON EVERYDAY SCIENCE

### *1. A candle*

"Here comes a candle to light you to bed!"

i. **The Shape.** The shape of a candle is worth noticing. It is cylindrical—every point on the outside edge is the same distance from the wick as every other point. This makes the candle burn evenly.

Some candles taper at the lower end. The advantage of this is that you can push the candle into the candlestick till it reaches a point where it fits firmly.

ii. **The wax. Experiment 1.** Put some candle wax (paraffin wax) on a tin lid and place it near the fire or over a gas flame turned low. Notice that the wax melts readily.

**Experiment 2.** Put a small splint of wood in the melted wax. Take it out and leave it till the wax hardens. Then light the splint at the gas flame. Notice that the wax melts before it catches fire.

**Experiment 3.** Dip a piece of writing-paper in

water. The water does not wet it at once. Now dip a piece of similar paper in the melted wax. The wax wets it much more quickly than the water. The reason is that the surface of the water can bear a greater strain than the surface of the melted wax—the paper can break through the surface of the wax more easily than through the surface of water.

**Experiment 4.** Cut off a few chips of wax and drop them into the melted wax. Notice that they sink. This shows that solid wax is heavier than melted wax, and therefore that wax expands when it melts.

Compare wax with water—solid water (ice) floats on liquid water and therefore when ice melts it takes up less room.

**Experiment 5.** Drop a piece of wax into water. Notice that it floats. This shows that paraffin wax is lighter than water.

Pour a little melted wax on water. It floats on the surface and hardens as a flat sheet. Wax is sometimes used in this way to seal bottles of fruit.

iii. **The wick.** It is convenient to use lamp-wick for the following experiments because it is larger than candle-wick.

**Experiment 6.** Set fire to a piece of wick. Notice that it burns quickly and that the flame is not very clear. Dip the wick in melted wax. It then burns with a clear flame. By dipping at intervals, it may be made to burn for some time.

**Experiment 7.** Put a little water in a jar or bottle

and colour it with permanganate of potash (ink will do). Support a piece of wick with the end dipping into the water. Notice how the water soaks up into the wick. In this way oil rises in the wick of a lamp or melted wax in the wick of a candle.

Place the end of a piece of wick in melted wax and notice how the wax rises.

**Experiment 8.** Place a piece of wick in a jar of water with one end hanging over the side. It will be seen that after a time water soaks up through the wick and drips from the end.

iv. **A lighted candle. Experiment 9.** Light a candle and watch how it burns. The wax in the wick burns first; the flame goes down; the wax round the wick melts and soaks up into the wick; the candle burns brightly.

**Experiment 10.** Drop some specks of dust into the melted wax and notice how they run up to the wick.

**Experiment 11.** Blow out the flame. Notice the smoke. Hold a lighted match in the smoke about an inch from the wick. The flame will run down the smoke to the wick. See how far away you can hold a lighted match to light the candle. Notice that the solid wax turns to a liquid and then to a gas before it burns.

**Experiment 12.** Weigh a candle. Let it burn for five minutes. Then weigh it again. Find what weight has been burnt. How long will the candle last?

v. **What becomes of the wax.** The candle wax burns away. But what becomes of it? The following experiments show that three things are formed, one a solid, one usually a liquid, and the third an invisible gas.

**Experiment 13.** Hold a piece of white paper over the candle flame and in the flame. It is best to move the paper about. Do not hold it long enough to catch fire. When you take away the paper, you will find it covered with soot. If you think this is caused by the paper scorching, rub it off and you will find the unscorched paper below.

**Experiment 14.** Hold a glass jar over the burning candle (a jam-jar will do). Mist forms on the sides. When the jar becomes heated the mist goes.

Water is formed when a candle burns.

**Experiment 15.** Place a kettle of cold water on a gas-ring, or a flask of cold water over a bunsen-burner. In each case, when the gas is lighted, the cold vessel is covered with drops of moisture. Water is also formed when gas burns. (This experiment should be done because the water is more easily seen than with a candle.)

**Experiment 16.** Hold a jar over the candle for a minute. Then pour in a little lime-water and shake it up. The lime-water turns "milky". This is a test for a gas called carbon dioxide. It shows that this gas is in the jar even though you cannot see it.

Shake up some lime-water in another jar. You will find that it does not turn milky. There is some carbon dioxide in the air but it is only a very small part.

Breathe into the jar and shake up again. The

lime-water turns milky, showing that we breathe out carbon dioxide.

vi. **Air is necessary for burning.** To show that air is necessary for burning shut off the supply of air.

**Experiment 17.** Light a candle. Place over it a glass jar so as to shut off the supply of air. Notice that the candle quickly goes out.

Repeat the experiment, but just before the candle goes out remove the jar. Notice how the candle burns up again.

## 2. *Tea-table Science*

"And thou, great Anna, whom three realms obey,
Dost sometimes counsel take and sometimes tea."

[Why not both together ?]

i. **Sugar in Tea.** Not every one takes sugar in tea, but you can experiment with a lump of sugar even if you do not drink the tea afterwards!

**Experiment 1.** Place a lump of sugar in a spoon and let a few drops of tea run into it. The tea quickly rises through the sugar. It rises in small spaces between the particles of sugar just as water rises in a narrow tube.

**Experiment 2.** Hold the sugar near the surface of the tea and notice how quickly it breaks up and dissolves. Drop a lump of sugar to the bottom. It takes longer to dissolve, and when it does dissolve you will see bubbles of air rise to the top. This air kept the tea from the sugar and so it did not dissolve so quickly.

**Experiment 3.** Drop a lump of sugar into cold water and notice how much longer it is in dissolving. Leave the cup quite still for some time and then taste the water at the top. You will find that the sugar takes some time to spread through the water. When you stir tea the sugar dissolves more quickly because fresh unsugared tea is continually being brought to the sugar.

ii. **The surface of the tea.** Examine the surface of the tea in a cup. You will find that it is not quite flat. Where it touches the cup the surface of the tea curves up slightly.

**Experiment 4.** Fill a cup brim full. Carefully drop a number of coins into it. You will find that you can add a good many coins before the tea flows over the edge. The surface of a liquid can bear a slight weight, and you will find that the surface of tea is strong enough to keep the tea piled up above the level of the cup. (Figure 66.)

Fig 66

Tea raised above the level of the rim of the cup

iii. **Cooling tea. Experiment 5.** Pour tea into two cups, one being flat and the other high. Taste the tea in each after leaving them for some time. The tea in the flat cup is cooler. This is because there is a larger surface for the tea to lose heat. (Figure 67.)

Fig 67

Small surface—
less radiation

Larger surface—
more radiation

Still larger surface—
still more radiation

**Experiment 6.** Pour some tea into a saucer where there is a still larger surface. Notice how quickly the tea loses its heat.

iv. **Keeping tea hot. Experiment 7.** If there is a silver tea-pot, touch it when it is full of hot tea. It feels very hot because heat easily passes through silver. There is usually a handle through which heat does not pass easily. The handle is not nearly so hot.

Compare the silver tea-pot with an earthenware pot through which heat does not pass so easily.

**Experiment 8.** Leave a pot of tea for ten minutes covered with a cosy. Notice how hot it is. Then try the effect of leaving the pot uncovered. It quickly loses its heat. The cosy is made of fluffy material through which heat does not pass quickly.

v. **Reflection from tea. Experiment 9.** When you look down into a cup of tea there is not much reflection.

Now bring your eye down till it is nearly on a level with the surface of the tea. You will find things reflected in the tea, and the more nearly you bring your eye to a level with the tea the clearer is the reflection. Light is reflected best when it just grazes the surface.

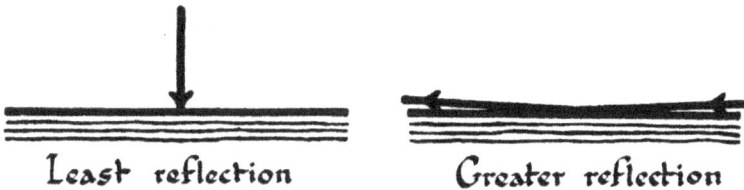

Least reflection          Greater reflection

**Experiment 10.** When the sun is shining, place a cup of tea, nearly full, so that the sun shines into it. You will find curves of light on the surface of the tea. These are caused by the reflection of the sun's rays from the part of the cup above the tea.

### 3. Science in the Home—1

**Ventilation. Experiment 1.** Close the doors, windows, chimney, and any other openings in a room. Notice how stuffy it soon becomes.

Open one window at the top and bottom. Hold a piece of smouldering paper near each opening. The smoke will show the direction of air currents—inward at the bottom and outward at the top.

Windows should be left open at both top and bottom for ventilation.

**Experiment 2.** The effect of a chimney in ventilating a room may be shown by holding a pipe over a gas-burner. A piece of iron drain-pipe about two inches across will do, or even a card-board tube.

Light the gas-burner and hold the tube over it. The rush of air into the tube from below may be so great as to blow out the gas flame.

**Dark and light rooms. Experiment 3.** Get a small box. (The sides may be eight or ten inches long, and it should be rather deep.)

Line the sides of the box with white paper. Cut out a paragraph from a newspaper or an old reading-book and put it at the bottom of the box. You should be able to read it quite easily.

Now line the box with brown paper. You will find that it is much darker at the bottom of the box.

Test other papers on the sides and bottom of the box, including the darkest paper you can get.

**Experiment 4.** Cover the sides and bottom of the box with a rather dark paper. Stand so that you can just read what is on the cutting in the box.

Get some one to reflect a beam of sunlight into the box from a mirror. The box will be lit up at once, and you will find that you can easily read what is on the cutting.

**Experiment 5.** Examine dark rooms, find out why they are dark, and how they can be made lighter.

i. Is the ceiling a light colour? Place a sheet of good white paper on the ceiling and compare the colours. Some "whites" are nearer black than white.

ii. Are the walls a light colour? Test the colour of walls on the reflection box. Light cream distemper is a good covering for dark rooms.

iii. What colour are the doors and other woodwork? These also should be a light colour.

iv. Is there much dark furniture in the room? If there is a dark table in the room, test the effect of covering it with a white cloth. You will find that the room is at once much lighter. (The dark table absorbs light; the white table-cloth reflects it.)

v. Examine the window or windows. Is there anything between the sky and the window that can be removed?

Test the effect of raising the blind as high as it will go. If there are dark hangings on the window, test the effect of removing these, and using only very light curtains pulled well away from the window.

vi. Stand outside the window and look up. Overhead there is usually bright sky. Some of this light may be thrown into the room by placing a reflector below the window at an angle of forty-five degrees with the level.

**Ornaments. Experiment 6.** Examine furniture and ornaments. Look for places where dust is likely to collect and where it cannot be removed easily. Simple surfaces and smooth curves are suitable for household purposes. Heavily carved and decorated surfaces act as dust traps. They encourage dirt and disease.

Anything which cannot easily be kept clean should be removed from places where people are to live.

It would be interesting to ask each thing in the room individually "What are you doing here?"

**Experiment 7.** Test whether ornaments are top-heavy by tilting them till they begin to fall. If the process is allowed to continue with really top-heavy vases there will be little loss.

**Resonance. Experiment 8.** Walk into an empty room. Notice the ringing sound. You may often notice this in rooms where there are few hangings. The reason is that sound is thrown from wall to wall and the whole air of the room is in movement.

Try the effect of spreading out a blanket in a room which resounds. The blanket will absorb the sound waves, and the resonance will cease. A carpet will have the same effect.

### 4. Science in the Home—2

**Gas-fires. Experiment 1.** Examine a gas-fire. Between the tap and the burner you will find a hole in the gas pipe. This hole is to admit air to burn the gas completely.L ight the gas and stop the air-hole with a piece of paper wrapped round the pipe. You will see that the flame changes from the blue flame to the yellow smoky flame.

If the gas-fire flame is yellow, examine the air-hole. See that it is clear and free from dirt. Sometimes the fire "roars." This is because the air-hole is too big. If there is no other way of adjusting the supply of air, a ring of metal may be used to cover the hole partly. (Cut a strip from a tin can and bend it round the pipe.)

**Experiment 2.** i. Examine a gas-oven. Find the air-hole. Look also for the ventilator near the top of the oven. Sometimes the gas keeps going out because the ventilator is choked up and insufficient air enters the oven to burn the gas. Test the effects of closing and of opening the ventilator when the gas is burning.

ii. The door and sides of the oven are packed with asbestos to check the escape of heat.

**Experiment 3.** i. Fill a small tin with water and find how long it takes to boil on a gas-ring.

ii. Find how long a similar tin of water takes to boil when the air-hole is covered. You will find that it takes longer to boil. You will see also that the yellow flame has made the tin sooty.

**Lighting a fire. Experiment 4.** Experiment in laying a fire.

i. Press the materials down tightly. You will find that it is almost impossible to light a fire like this.

ii. Arrange the materials loosely so that air can get at all parts of the fire. Put loosely squeezed up paper at the bottom, then dry sticks crossed so as to allow air between them, and coal placed loosely on the top.

iii. If a fire is burning badly, poke it to admit more air.

**Experiment 5.** i. When a fire is first lit, notice that a little smoke sometimes comes into the room. As the chimney becomes warmer, the stream of air through the chimney carries the smoke with it.

ii. Hold a sheet of tin in front of the fire so as to cover the space above the fire. The stream of air now passes through the fire and makes it blaze strongly.

iii. Notice that a fire heats things by radiating heat. Stand near the fire. You can feel the heat of the fire even when the air is quite fresh.

Close doors and windows for a short time and notice how stuffy the room feels when the air has become warm and stale.

Notice also the advantage of having the fire well forward into the room so that as much heat as possible is radiated into the room. In a gas-fire fire-clay is used to give a big radiating surface.

**Good conductors of heat.** Good conductors of heat are used in the kitchen where things are to be heated. Kettles are made of copper or iron ("tin" kettles are iron, covered with tin to prevent rusting).

**Experiment 6.** Fill a tin lid with water and place it over a small gas-ring. Find how long it takes to boil.

Fill the lid again, place it on a larger lid full of soot, and see how long it takes to boil. You will see that it takes much longer.

Kettles and pans should be kept free from soot. If they are sooty, water takes longer to boil in them.

**Bad conductors of heat.** Bad conductors of heat are used for lifting hot things or for keeping things hot.

Make a note of things used in this way, e.g. kettle-holders made of fluffy material (paper will do very well), ebonite handles of silver tea-pots, tea-cosies, blankets.

Note also the sides of a gas-oven, and hay-boxes.

www.ingramcontent.com/pod-product-compliance
Lightning Source LLC
LaVergne TN
LVHW011234080426
835509LV00005B/494